Especially for

Me
_____

From

Roz Burr
_____

Date

12/11/2014
_____
Jackie's First Fifty

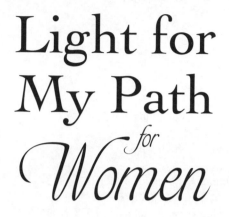

Light for My Path for Women

Scriptures to Illuminate Your Life

BARBOUR
PUBLISHING

© 2007 by Barbour Publishing, Inc.

Print ISBN 978-1-62416-249-7

eBook Editions:
Adobe Digital Edition (.epub) 978-1-62416-461-3
Kindle and MobiPocket Edition (.prc) 978-1-62416-460-6

All scripture quotations are taken from the King James Version of the
Bible.

Published by Barbour Publishing Inc., P.O. Box 719, Uhrichsville,
Ohio 44683, www.barbourbooks.com

*Our mission is to publish and distribute inspirational products offering
exceptional value and biblical encouragement to the masses.*

ecpa Member of the
Evangelical Christian
Publishers Association

Printed in China.

Contents

Introduction

Our world sends many conflicting signals on the important issues of life. How should we approach anger? Is discipline a good thing or not? Why speak with honesty? Is prayer for real? What is true wisdom?

In His kindness, God has answered all of these questions—and many more—in the pages of His Word, the Bible. Whatever our needs, we can find in scripture the principles we need to address the issues we face.

This collection of Bible verses is a handy reference to some of the key issues that all people—and especially women—face. In these pages, you'll find carefully selected verses that address topics like comfort, encouragement, friendship, purity, rest, and understanding. In fact, more than four dozen categories are covered, arranged alphabetically for ease of use.

This book is not intended to replace regular, personal Bible study. Nor is it a replacement for a good concordance for in-depth study of a particular subject. It is, however, a quick reference to some of the key issues of life that women most often face. We hope it will be an encouragement to you as you read.

All scripture is taken from the King James Version of the Bible.

Adversity

*Our Creator never intended that we
should shoulder a load of suffering ourselves.
That's the whole purpose of spiritual community.*
LINDA BARTLETT

For I reckon that the sufferings of this present time are not worthy to be compared with the glory which shall be revealed in us.

ROMANS 8:18

For as the sufferings of Christ abound in us, so our consolation also aboundeth by Christ. And whether we be afflicted, it is for your consolation and salvation, which is effectual in the enduring of the same sufferings which we also suffer: or whether we be comforted, it is for your consolation and salvation.

2 CORINTHIANS 1:5–6

If ye be reproached for the name of Christ, happy are ye; for the spirit of glory and of God resteth upon you: on their part he is evil spoken of, but on your part he is glorified.

1 PETER 4:14

These things I have spoken unto you, that in me ye might have peace. In the world ye shall have tribulation: but be of good cheer; I have overcome the world.

JOHN 16:33

But the God of all grace, who hath called us unto his eternal glory by Christ Jesus, after that ye have suffered a while, make you perfect, stablish, strengthen, settle you.

1 PETER 5:10

That the trial of your faith, being much more precious than of gold that perisheth, though it be tried with fire, might be found unto praise and honour and glory at the appearing of Jesus Christ.

1 PETER 1:7

The righteous cry, and the LORD heareth, and delivereth them out of all their troubles.

PSALM 34:17

Blessed are ye, when men shall hate you, and when they shall separate you from their company, and shall reproach you, and cast out your name as evil, for the Son of man's sake.

LUKE 6:22

Is any among you afflicted? let him pray.

JAMES 5:13

Yea, and all that will live godly in Christ Jesus shall suffer persecution.

2 TIMOTHY 3:12

Beloved, think it not strange concerning the fiery trial which is to try you, as though some strange thing happened unto you: but rejoice, inasmuch as ye are partakers of Christ's sufferings; that, when his glory shall be revealed, ye may be glad also with exceeding joy.

1 PETER 4:12–13

Heavenly Father,
*I feel the darkness encompassing me. The burden is so heavy to bear.
I thank You that You have promised to take this weight from me.
I will surrender it to You, leaving it in Your loving hands. Amen.*

Anger

*Being angry or unforgiving makes it
impossible to have a gentle and quiet spirit.*
DARLENE WILKINSON

He that is slow to wrath is of great understanding: but he that is
hasty of spirit exalteth folly.

PROVERBS 14:29

Wherefore, my beloved brethren, let every man be swift to hear,
slow to speak, slow to wrath: for the wrath of man worketh
not the righteousness of God.

JAMES 1:19–20

Make no friendship with an angry man; and with a furious man
thou shalt not go: lest thou learn his ways, and get a snare to
thy soul.

PROVERBS 22:24–25

Be not hasty in thy spirit to be angry: for anger resteth in the
bosom of fools.

ECCLESIASTES 7:9

A wrathful man stirreth up strife: but he that is slow to anger
appeaseth strife.

PROVERBS 15:18

It is better to dwell in the wilderness, than with a contentious
and an angry woman.

PROVERBS 21:19

Fathers, provoke not your children to anger, lest they be discouraged.

COLOSSIANS 3:21

A soft answer turneth away wrath: but grievous words stir up anger.

PROVERBS 15:1

But I say unto you, That whosoever is angry with his brother without a cause shall be in danger of the judgment: and whosoever shall say to his brother, Raca, shall be in danger of the council: but whosoever shall say, Thou fool, shall be in danger of hell fire.

MATTHEW 5:22

He that is slow to anger is better than the mighty and he that ruleth his spirit than he that taketh a city.

PROVERBS 16:32

Dearly beloved, avenge not yourselves, but rather give place unto wrath: for it is written, Vengeance is mine; I will repay, saith the Lord.

ROMANS 12:19

Do all things without murmurings and disputings.

PHILIPPIANS 2:14

Be ye angry, and sin not: let not the sun go down upon your wrath.

EPHESIANS 4:26

Father,
*I didn't keep my anger in check. I'm sorry that I failed You.
Please help me to guard my tongue so that I don't
use harsh words to inflict pain on others. Amen.*

Charity

Charity begins at home.
PROVERB

He that despiseth his neighbour sinneth: but he that hath mercy
on the poor, happy is he.

PROVERBS 14:21

Blessed is he that considereth the poor: the LORD will deliver him
in time of trouble. The LORD will preserve him, and keep him
alive; and he shall be blessed upon the earth: and thou wilt not
deliver him unto the will of his enemies.

PSALM 41:1–2

He that hath pity upon the poor lendeth unto the LORD; and
that which he hath given will he pay him again.

PROVERBS 19:17

I have shewed you all things, how that so labouring ye ought to
support the weak, and to remember the words of the Lord Jesus,
how he said, It is more blessed to give than to receive.

ACTS 20:35

Charge them that are rich in this world, that they be not
highminded, nor trust in uncertain riches, but in the living
God, who giveth us richly all things to enjoy; that they do good,
that they be rich in good works, ready to distribute, willing to
communicate; laying up in store for themselves a good foundation
against the time to come, that they may lay hold on eternal life.

1 TIMOTHY 6:17–19

But when thou makest a feast, call the poor, the maimed, the lame, the blind: and thou shalt be blessed; for they cannot recompense thee: for thou shalt be recompensed at the resurrection of the just.

LUKE 14:13–14

I have been young, and now am old; yet have I not seen the righteous forsaken, nor his seed begging bread. He is ever merciful, and lendeth; and his seed is blessed.

PSALM 37:25–26

Sell that ye have, and give alms; provide yourselves bags which wax not old, a treasure in the heavens that faileth not, where no thief approacheth, neither moth corrupteth. For where your treasure is, there will your heart be also.

LUKE 12:33–34

He hath dispersed, he hath given to the poor; his righteousness endureth for ever.

PSALM 112:9

Above all things have fervent charity among yourselves: for charity shall cover the multitude of sins. Use hospitality one to another without grudging. As every man hath received the gift, even so minister the same one to another, as good stewards of the manifold grace of God.

1 PETER 4:8–10

Give, and it shall be given unto you; good measure, pressed down, and shaken together, and running over, shall men give into your bosom. For with the same measure that ye mete withal it shall be measured to you again.

LUKE 6:38

Thank You, Lord,
for all of the blessings You have given to me. You have made me responsible for these blessings, but they ultimately belong to You. Help me to share them with others. Amen.

Comfort

*All you really need is the One who promised never to leave
or forsake you—the One who said, "Lo, I am with you always."*
JONI EARECKSON TADA

Casting all your care upon him; for he careth for you.

1 PETER 5:7

Yea, though I walk through the valley of the shadow of death, I
will fear no evil: for thou art with me; thy rod and thy staff they
comfort me.

PSALM 23:4

And God shall wipe away all tears from their eyes; and there shall
be no more death, neither sorrow, nor crying, neither shall there
be any more pain: for the former things are passed away.

REVELATION 21:4

The Lord GOD will wipe away tears from off all faces.

ISAIAH 25:8

For the Lord himself shall descend from heaven with a shout,
with the voice of the archangel, and with the trump of God: and
the dead in Christ shall rise first: then we which are alive and
remain shall be caught up together with them in the clouds to
meet the Lord in the air: and so shall we ever be with the Lord.
Wherefore comfort one another with these words.

1 THESSALONIANS 4:16–18

Comfort ye, comfort ye my people, saith your God.

ISAIAH 40:1

In the multitude of my thoughts within me thy comforts delight my soul.

PSALM 94:19

Blessed be God, even the Father of our Lord Jesus Christ, the Father of mercies, and the God of all comfort; who comforteth us in all our tribulation, that we may be able to comfort them which are in any trouble, by the comfort wherewith we ourselves are comforted of God. For as the sufferings of Christ abound in us, so our consolation also aboundeth by Christ.

2 CORINTHIANS 1:3–5

Blessed are they that mourn: for they shall be comforted.

MATTHEW 5:4

Thou shalt increase my greatness, and comfort me on every side.

PSALM 71:21

And, lo, I am with you always, even unto the end of the world.

MATTHEW 28:20

And I will pray the Father, and he shall give you another Comforter, that he may abide with you for ever.

JOHN 14:16

I will not leave you comfortless: I will come to you.

JOHN 14:18

Come unto me, all ye that labour and are heavy laden, and I will give you rest.

MATTHEW 11:28

As one whom his mother comforteth, so will I comfort you.

ISAIAH 66:13

I remembered thy judgments of old, O LORD; and have
comforted myself.

PSALM 119:52

Be perfect, be of good comfort, be of one mind, live in peace;
and the God of love and peace shall be with you.

2 CORINTHIANS 13:11

Draw nigh to God, and he will draw nigh to you.

JAMES 4:8

Dear God,
*thank You for sending Your Comforter to soothe my hurting.
I don't need to look to earthly friends for help, although You have
given those who support me in the worst of times. You are always
just a prayer away, and even when I can't think of the right words,
You still understand me. Thank You, Lord. Amen.*

Counsel

*The true secret of giving advice is, after you have honestly
given it, to be perfectly indifferent whether it is taken
or not, and never persist in trying to set people right.*
HANNAH WHITALL SMITH

As every man hath received the gift, even so minister the same
one to another, as good stewards of the manifold grace of God.

1 PETER 4:10

For unto us a child is born, unto us a son is given: and the
government shall be upon his shoulder: and his name shall be
called Wonderful, Counsellor, The mighty God, The everlasting
Father, The Prince of Peace.

ISAIAH 9:6

Hear counsel, and receive instruction, that thou mayest be wise
in thy latter end.

PROVERBS 19:20

Now no chastening for the present seemeth to be joyous, but
grievous: nevertheless afterward it yieldeth the peaceable fruit of
righteousness unto them which are exercised thereby.

HEBREWS 12:11

Howbeit when he, the Spirit of truth, is come, he will guide you
into all truth: for he shall not speak of himself; but whatsoever
he shall hear, that shall he speak: and he will shew you things to
come.

JOHN 16:13

And all thy children shall be taught of the LORD; and great shall be the peace of thy children.

ISAIAH 54:13

Give instruction to a wise man, and he will be yet wiser: teach a just man, and he will increase in learning.

PROVERBS 9:9

Brethren, if a man be overtaken in a fault, ye which are spiritual, restore such an one in the spirit of meekness; considering thyself, lest thou also be tempted.

GALATIANS 6:1

The way of a fool is right in his own eyes: but he that hearkeneth unto counsel is wise.

PROVERBS 12:15

Ointment and perfume rejoice the heart: so doth the sweetness of a man's friend by hearty counsel.

PROVERBS 27:9

For whom the Lord loveth he chasteneth, and scourgeth every son whom he receiveth. If ye endure chastening, God dealeth with you as with sons; for what son is he whom the father chasteneth not?

HEBREWS 12:6–7

Dear God,
*I pray that I won't be too proud to ask for help and advice
from others. Please let me be receptive to their words.
When others come to me for counsel, give me ears to
listen and the right words to respond. Amen.*

Courage

*You have to accept whatever comes and the only
important thing is that you meet it with courage,
and with the best you have to give.*
ELEANOR ROOSEVELT

And now, little children, abide in him; that, when he shall
appear, we may have confidence, and not be ashamed before him
at his coming.

1 JOHN 2:28

Only be thou strong and very courageous, that thou mayest
observe to do according to all the law, which Moses my servant
commanded thee: turn not from it to the right hand or to the
left, that thou mayest prosper whithersoever thou goest.

JOSHUA 1:7

Wait on the LORD: be of good courage, and he shall strengthen
thine heart: wait, I say, on the LORD.

PSALM 27:14

For God hath not given us the spirit of fear; but of power, and of
love, and of a sound mind.

2 TIMOTHY 1:7

So that we may boldly say, The LORD is my helper, and I will not
fear what man shall do unto me.

HEBREWS 13:6

In the fear of the LORD is strong confidence: and his children
shall have a place of refuge.

PROVERBS 14:26

Watch ye, stand fast in the faith, quit you like men, be strong.

1 CORINTHIANS 16:13

The wicked flee when no man pursueth: but the righteous are bold as a lion.

PROVERBS 28:1

Having therefore, brethren, boldness to enter into the holiest by the blood of Jesus.

HEBREWS 10:19

Be of good courage, and he shall strengthen your heart, all ye that hope in the LORD.

PSALM 31:24

In whom we have boldness and access with confidence by the faith of him.

EPHESIANS 3:12

Father,
forgive me when I'm fearful. I know that You are bigger than anything I may encounter in life. Remind me that You have laid out my future, and You already know what is going to happen. I confess my apprehensions. Amen.

Diligence

*When I stand before God at the end of my life, I would hope that
I would not have a single bit of talent left and could say,
"I used everything you gave me."*
ERMA BOMBECK

I call to remembrance my song in the night: I commune with
mine own heart: and my spirit made diligent search.

PSALM 77:6

But take diligent heed to do the commandment and the law,
which Moses the servant of the LORD charged you, to love the
LORD your God, and to walk in all his ways, and to keep his
commandments, and to cleave unto him, and to serve him with all
your heart and with all your soul.

JOSHUA 22:5

Therefore, as ye abound in every thing, in faith, and utterance,
and knowledge, and in all diligence, and in your love to us,
see that ye abound in this grace also.

2 CORINTHIANS 8:7

Keep thy heart with all diligence; for out of it are the issues of life.

PROVERBS 4:23

The soul of the sluggard desireth, and hath nothing: but the soul
of the diligent shall be made fat.

PROVERBS 13:4

And beside this, giving all diligence, add to your faith virtue;
and to virtue knowledge; and to knowledge temperance; and to
temperance patience; and to patience godliness; and to godliness

brotherly kindness; and to brotherly kindness charity. . . .
Wherefore the rather, brethren, give diligence to make your calling
and election sure: for if ye do these things, ye shall never fall.

2 PETER 1:5–7, 10

Labour not for the meat which perisheth, but for that meat
which endureth unto everlasting life, which the Son of man shall
give unto you: for him hath God the Father sealed.

JOHN 6:27

Behold that which I have seen: it is good and comely for one
to eat and to drink, and to enjoy the good of all his labour
that he taketh under the sun all the days of his life, which God
giveth him: for it is his portion. Every man also to whom God
hath given riches and wealth, and hath given him power to eat
thereof, and to take his portion, and to rejoice in his labour; this
is the gift of God.

ECCLESIASTES 5:18–19

I must work the works of him that sent me, while it is day: the
night cometh, when no man can work.

JOHN 9:4

He becometh poor that dealeth with a slack hand: but the hand
of the diligent maketh rich.

PROVERBS 10:4

But ye, brethren, be not weary in well doing.

2 THESSALONIANS 3:13

Or he that exhorteth, on exhortation: he that giveth, let him do
it with simplicity; he that ruleth, with diligence; he that sheweth
mercy, with cheerfulness.

ROMANS 12:8

And let us not be weary in well doing: for in due season we shall reap, if we faint not.

GALATIANS 6:9

Wherefore, beloved, seeing that ye look for such things, be diligent that ye may be found of him in peace, without spot, and blameless.

2 PETER 3:14

Whatsoever is commanded by the God of heaven, let it be diligently done for the house of the God of heaven: for why should there be wrath against the realm of the king and his sons?

EZRA 7:23

Therefore, my beloved brethren, be ye stedfast, unmoveable, always abounding in the work of the Lord, forasmuch as ye know that your labour is not in vain in the Lord.

1 CORINTHIANS 15:58

The thoughts of the diligent tend only to plenteousness; but of every one that is hasty only to want.

PROVERBS 21:5

Much food is in the tillage of the poor: but there is that is destroyed for want of judgment.

PROVERBS 13:23

Thank You

for opportunities, Jesus. Day by day through study and work,
help me to reach higher levels of character. In my climb,
Lord, guide me to great heights. Amen.

Encouragement

What men and women need is encouragement. . . .
Instead of always harping on a man's faults, tell him
of his virtues. Try to pull him out of his rut of bad habits.
ELEANOR H. PORTER

But exhort one another daily, while it is called To day; lest any of you be hardened through the deceitfulness of sin.

HEBREWS 3:13

Holding fast the faithful word as he hath been taught, that he may be able by sound doctrine both to exhort and to convince the gainsayers.

TITUS 1:9

Confirming the souls of the disciples, and exhorting them to continue in the faith, and that we must through much tribulation enter into the kingdom of God.

ACTS 14:22

Not forsaking the assembling of ourselves together, as the manner of some is; but exhorting one another: and so much the more, as ye see the day approaching.

HEBREWS 10:25

Therefore, brethren, stand fast, and hold the traditions which ye have been taught, whether by word, or our epistle. Now our Lord Jesus Christ himself, and God, even our Father, which hath loved us, and hath given us everlasting consolation and good hope through grace, comfort your hearts, and stablish you in every good word and work.

2 THESSALONIANS 2:15–17

He giveth power to the faint; and to them that have no might he increaseth strength.

ISAIAH 40:29

And when they bring you unto the synagogues, and unto magistrates, and powers, take ye no thought how or what thing ye shall answer, or what ye shall say: for the Holy Ghost shall teach you in the same hour what ye ought to say.

LUKE 12:11–12

Wherefore comfort yourselves together, and edify one another, even as also ye do.

1 THESSALONIANS 5:11

I can do all things through Christ which strengtheneth me.

PHILIPPIANS 4:13

And whether we be afflicted, it is for your consolation and salvation, which is effectual in the enduring of the same sufferings which we also suffer: or whether we be comforted, it is for your consolation and salvation.

2 CORINTHIANS 1:6

All scripture is given by inspiration of God, and is profitable for doctrine, for reproof, for correction, for instruction in righteousness.

2 TIMOTHY 3:16

Brethren, if any of you do err from the truth, and one convert him; let him know, that he which converteth the sinner from the error of his way shall save a soul from death, and shall hide a multitude of sins.

JAMES 5:19–20

Bear ye one another's burdens, and so fulfil the law of Christ.

GALATIANS 6:2

Lord Jesus,
thank You for the encouraging words that others have for me.
I pray that I will be an encouragement to others as well. Amen.

Eternity

Redeemed, how I love to proclaim it!
His child, and forever, I am.
FANNY CROSBY

In my Father's house are many mansions: if it were not so, I
would have told you. I go to prepare a place for you. And if I go
and prepare a place for you, I will come again, and receive you
unto myself; that where I am, there ye may be also.

JOHN 14:2–3

Henceforth there is laid up for me a crown of righteousness, which
the LORD, the righteous judge, shall give me at that day: and not to
me only, but unto all them also that love his appearing.

2 TIMOTHY 4:8

He that loveth his life shall lose it; and he that hateth his life in
this world shall keep it unto life eternal.

JOHN 12:25

And I saw a new heaven and a new earth: for the first heaven and
the first earth were passed away; and there was no more sea. And
I John saw the holy city, new Jerusalem, coming down from God
out of heaven, prepared as a bride adorned for her husband.

REVELATION 21:1–2

For the wages of sin is death; but the gift of God is eternal life
through Jesus Christ our Lord.

ROMANS 6:23

And he saith unto them, Ye shall drink indeed of my cup, and be baptized with the baptism that I am baptized with: but to sit on my right hand, and on my left, is not mine to give, but it shall be given to them for whom it is prepared of my Father.

MATTHEW 20:23

And I give unto them eternal life; and they shall never perish, neither shall any man pluck them out of my hand.

JOHN 10:28

For we know that if our earthly house of this tabernacle were dissolved, we have a building of God, an house not made with hands, eternal in the heavens.

2 CORINTHIANS 5:1

Behold, I shew you a mystery; We shall not all sleep, but we shall all be changed, in a moment, in the twinkling of an eye, at the last trump: for the trumpet shall sound, and the dead shall be raised incorruptible, and we shall be changed. For this corruptible must put on incorruption, and this mortal must put on immortality. So when this corruptible shall have put on incorruption, and this mortal shall have put on immortality, then shall be brought to pass the saying that is written, Death is swallowed up in victory.

1 CORINTHIANS 15:51–54

Nevertheless we, according to his promise, look for new heavens and a new earth, wherein dwelleth righteousness.

2 PETER 3:13

He that soweth to the Spirit shall of the Spirit reap life everlasting.

GALATIANS 6:8

And when the chief Shepherd shall appear, ye shall receive a
crown of glory that fadeth not away.

1 PETER 5:4

And many of them that sleep in the dust of the earth shall awake,
some to everlasting life, and some to shame and everlasting
contempt.

DANIEL 12:2

Jesus said unto her, I am the resurrection, and the life: he that
believeth in me, though he were dead, yet shall he live: and
whosoever liveth and believeth in me shall never die. Believest
thou this?

JOHN 11:25–26

Search the scriptures; for in them ye think ye have eternal life:
and they are they which testify of me.

JOHN 5:39

God. . .will render to every man according to his deeds: to them
who by patient continuance in well doing seek for glory and
honour and immortality, eternal life.

ROMANS 2:5–7

Labour not for the meat which perisheth, but for that meat
which endureth unto everlasting life, which the Son of man shall
give unto you: for him hath God the Father sealed.

JOHN 6:27

But if the Spirit of him that raised up Jesus from the dead
dwell in you, he that raised up Christ from the dead shall also
quicken your mortal bodies by his Spirit that dwelleth in you.

ROMANS 8:11

And there shall be no night there; and they need no candle, neither light of the sun; for the Lord God giveth them light: and they shall reign for ever and ever.

REVELATION 22:5

Verily, verily, I say unto you, He that heareth my word, and believeth on him that sent me, hath everlasting life, and shall not come into condemnation; but is passed from death unto life.

JOHN 5:24

Blessed be the God and Father of our Lord Jesus Christ, which according to his abundant mercy hath begotten us again unto a lively hope by the resurrection of Jesus Christ from the dead, to an inheritance incorruptible, and undefiled, and that fadeth not away, reserved in heaven for you, who are kept by the power of God through faith unto salvation ready to be revealed in the last time.

1 PETER 1:3–5

Therefore are they before the throne of God, and serve him day and night in his temple: and he that sitteth on the throne shall dwell among them. They shall hunger no more, neither thirst any more; neither shall the sun light on them, nor any heat. For the Lamb which is in the midst of the throne shall feed them, and shall lead them unto living fountains of waters: and God shall wipe away all tears from their eyes.

REVELATION 7:15–17

Lord God,

I feel so special when I think that You are preparing a place in heaven for me. To be considered Your child is overwhelming, as You have chosen me to be a part of Your family. I long to be in Your presence, laying my crown at Your feet, and worshipping You forever. Amen.

Faith

*Faith sees the invisible, believes the unbelievable,
and receives the impossible.*
CORRIE TEN BOOM

Ask in faith, nothing wavering. For he that wavereth is like a
wave of the sea driven with the wind and tossed.

JAMES 1:6

And the Lord said, If ye had faith as a grain of mustard seed, ye
might say unto this sycamine tree, Be thou plucked up by the
root, and be thou planted in the sea; and it should obey you.

LUKE 17:6

Whom having not seen, ye love; in whom, though now ye see
him not, yet believing, ye rejoice with joy unspeakable and full
of glory.

1 PETER 1:8

That if thou shalt confess with thy mouth the Lord Jesus, and
shalt believe in thine heart that God hath raised him from the
dead, thou shalt be saved.

ROMANS 10:9

As soon as Jesus heard the word that was spoken, he saith unto
the ruler of the synagogue, Be not afraid, only believe.

MARK 5:36

And he said to the woman, Thy faith hath saved thee; go in
peace.

LUKE 7:50

For ye are all the children of God by faith in Christ Jesus.

GALATIANS 3:26

But as many as received him, to them gave he power to become the sons of God, even to them that believe on his name.

JOHN 1:12

He that believeth and is baptized shall be saved; but he that believeth not shall be damned.

MARK 16:16

Now faith is the substance of things hoped for, the evidence of things not seen.

HEBREWS 11:1

That Christ may dwell in your hearts by faith; that ye, being rooted and grounded in love, may be able to comprehend with all saints what is the breadth, and length, and depth, and height; and to know the love of Christ, which passeth knowledge, that ye might be filled with all the fulness of God.

EPHESIANS 3:17–19

Jesus said unto him, If thou canst believe, all things are possible to him that believeth.

MARK 9:23

It is written in the prophets, And they shall be all taught of God. Every man therefore that hath heard, and hath learned of the Father, cometh unto me.

JOHN 6:45

That your faith should not stand in the wisdom of men, but in the power of God.

1 CORINTHIANS 2:5

Watch ye, stand fast in the faith, quit you like men, be strong.

1 Corinthians 16:13

And Jesus answering saith unto them, Have faith in God. For verily I say unto you, That whosoever shall say unto this mountain, Be thou removed, and be thou cast into the sea; and shall not doubt in his heart, but shall believe that those things which he saith shall come to pass; he shall have whatsoever he saith.

Mark 11:22–23

For by grace are ye saved through faith; and that not of yourselves: it is the gift of God.

Ephesians 2:8

Jesus saith unto him, Thomas, because thou hast seen me, thou hast believed: blessed are they that have not seen, and yet have believed.

John 20:29

But without faith it is impossible to please him: for he that cometh to God must believe that he is, and that he is a rewarder of them that diligently seek him.

Hebrews 11:6

Jesus answered and said unto them, This is the work of God, that ye believe on him whom he hath sent.

John 6:29

Let us draw near with a true heart in full assurance of faith, having our hearts sprinkled from an evil conscience, and our bodies washed with pure water.

Hebrews 10:22

He that believeth on the Son of God hath the witness in himself: he that believeth not God hath made him a liar; because he believeth not the record that God gave of his Son.

1 JOHN 5:10

As ye have therefore received Christ Jesus the Lord, so walk ye in him.

COLOSSIANS 2:6

Behold, I stand at the door, and knock: if any man hear my voice, and open the door, I will come in to him, and will sup with him, and he with me.

REVELATION 3:20

Jesus saith unto her, Said I not unto thee, that, if thou wouldest believe, thou shouldest see the glory of God?

JOHN 11:40

The life which I now live in the flesh I live by the faith of the Son of God, who loved me, and gave himself for me.

GALATIANS 2:20

For we walk by faith, not by sight.

2 CORINTHIANS 5:7

Father,
please help me to be a woman of faith, believing that You will work all details out in my life. Let me not rely on tangible, explainable things, but to remember that You are in control of everything— known and unknown. Amen.

Faithfulness of God

*God's designs regarding you, and His methods of
bringing about these designs, are infinitely wise.*
MADAME GUYON

And we know that all things work together for good to them that
love God, to them who are the called according to his purpose.

ROMANS 8:28

And the heavens shall praise thy wonders, O LORD: thy
faithfulness also in the congregation of the saints.

PSALM 89:5

A faithful man shall abound with blessings: but he that maketh
haste to be rich shall not be innocent.

PROVERBS 28:20

Who then is a faithful and wise servant, whom his lord hath
made ruler over his household, to give them meat in due season?
Blessed is that servant, whom his lord when he cometh shall find
so doing. Verily I say unto you, That he shall make him ruler
over all his goods.

MATTHEW 24:45–47

In hope of eternal life, which God, that cannot lie, promised
before the world began.

TITUS 1:2

Therefore thus saith the Lord GOD, Behold, I lay in Zion for a
foundation a stone, a tried stone, a precious corner stone, a sure
foundation; he that believeth shall not make haste.

ISAIAH 28:16

If we believe not, yet he abideth faithful: he cannot deny himself.

2 TIMOTHY 2:13

The Lord is not slack concerning his promise, as some men count slackness; but is longsuffering to us-ward, not willing that any should perish, but that all should come to repentance.

2 PETER 3:9

(For the LORD thy God is a merciful God;) he will not forsake thee, neither destroy thee, nor forget the covenant of thy fathers which he sware unto them.

DEUTERONOMY 4:31

God is not a man, that he should lie; neither the son of man, that he should repent: hath he said, and shall he not do it? or hath he spoken, and shall he not make it good?

NUMBERS 23:19

Blessed be the LORD, that hath given rest unto his people Israel, according to all that he promised: there hath not failed one word of all his good promise, which he promised by the hand of Moses his servant.

1 KINGS 8:56

Let us hold fast the profession of our faith without wavering; (for he is faithful that promised).

HEBREWS 10:23

O love the LORD, all ye his saints: for the LORD preserveth the faithful, and plentifully rewardeth the proud doer.

PSALM 31:23

Know therefore that the LORD thy God, he is God, the faithful God, which keepeth covenant and mercy with them that love him and keep his commandments to a thousand generations.

DEUTERONOMY 7:9

Be thou faithful unto death, and I will give thee a crown of life.

REVELATION 2:10

Thank You, Lord,
for remaining steadfast. Nothing else in my life is as sure as You.
I am grateful that You will never leave me, regardless of what I do.
I love You, Lord! Amen.

Fearing God

*Reverence for the Lord is
the beginning of wisdom.*
ELISABETH ELLIOT

And fear not them which kill the body, but are not able to kill
the soul: but rather fear him which is able to destroy both soul
and body in hell.

MATTHEW 10:28

Moreover thou shalt provide out of all the people able men, such
as fear God, men of truth, hating covetousness; and place such
over them, to be rulers of thousands, and rulers of hundreds,
rulers of fifties, and rulers of tens.

EXODUS 18:21

The fear of the LORD is the beginning of knowledge: but fools
despise wisdom and instruction.

PROVERBS 1:7

Saying with a loud voice, Fear God, and give glory to him; for
the hour of his judgment is come: and worship him that made
heaven, and earth, and the sea, and the fountains of waters.

REVELATION 14:7

O that there were such an heart in them, that they would fear
me, and keep all my commandments always, that it might be
well with them, and with their children for ever!

DEUTERONOMY 5:29

The angel of the LORD encampeth round about them that fear him, and delivereth them.

PSALM 34:7

Thou believest that there is one God; thou doest well: the devils also believe, and tremble.

JAMES 2:19

Only fear the LORD, and serve him in truth with all your heart: for consider how great things he hath done for you.

1 SAMUEL 12:24

A wise man feareth, and departeth from evil: but the fool rageth, and is confident.

PROVERBS 14:16

Wherefore we receiving a kingdom which cannot be moved, let us have grace, whereby we may serve God acceptably with reverence and godly fear: for our God is a consuming fire.

HEBREWS 12:28–29

Wherefore, my beloved, as ye have always obeyed, not as in my presence only, but now much more in my absence, work out your own salvation with fear and trembling.

PHILIPPIANS 2:12

Men do therefore fear him: he respecteth not any that are wise of heart.

JOB 37:24

Serve the LORD with fear, and rejoice with trembling.

PSALM 2:11

Having therefore these promises, dearly beloved, let us cleanse ourselves from all filthiness of the flesh and spirit, perfecting holiness in the fear of God.

2 Corinthians 7:1

He will fulfil the desire of them that fear him: he also will hear their cry, and will save them.

Psalm 145:19

The fear of the Lord is to hate evil: pride, and arrogancy, and the evil way, and the froward mouth, do I hate.

Proverbs 8:13

Let us hear the conclusion of the whole matter: Fear God, and keep his commandments: for this is the whole duty of man.

Ecclesiastes 12:13

Fear ye not me? saith the Lord: will ye not tremble at my presence, which have placed the sand for the bound of the sea by a perpetual decree, that it cannot pass it: and though the waves thereof toss themselves, yet can they not prevail; though they roar, yet can they not pass over it?

Jeremiah 5:22

Then they that feared the Lord spake often one to another: and the Lord hearkened, and heard it, and a book of remembrance was written before him for them that feared the Lord, and that thought upon his name.

Malachi 3:16

Lord God,
You are holy. You can control anything with a mere whisper.
Yet You love me and are patient with me. Thank You, Father! Amen.

Forgiveness

*If the wounds of millions are to be healed,
what other way is there except through forgiveness?*
CATHERINE MARSHALL

And be ye kind one to another, tenderhearted, forgiving one
another, even as God for Christ's sake hath forgiven you.

EPHESIANS 4:32

Forbearing one another, and forgiving one another, if any man
have a quarrel against any: even as Christ forgave you, so also
do ye.

COLOSSIANS 3:13

Not rendering evil for evil, or railing for railing: but contrariwise
blessing; knowing that ye are thereunto called, that ye should
inherit a blessing.

1 PETER 3:9

And forgive us our debts, as we forgive our debtors.

MATTHEW 6:12

For if ye forgive men their trespasses, your heavenly Father
will also forgive you: But if ye forgive not men their trespasses,
neither will your Father forgive your trespasses.

MATTHEW 6:14–15

And forgive us our sins; for we also forgive every one that is
indebted to us. And lead us not into temptation; but deliver us
from evil.

LUKE 11:4

Then came Peter to him, and said, Lord, how oft shall my brother sin against me, and I forgive him? till seven times? Jesus saith unto him, I say not unto thee, Until seven times: but, Until seventy times seven.

MATTHEW 18:21–22

Take heed to yourselves: If thy brother trespass against thee, rebuke him; and if he repent, forgive him. And if he trespass against thee seven times in a day, and seven times in a day turn again to thee, saying, I repent; thou shalt forgive him.

LUKE 17:3–4

And when ye stand praying, forgive, if ye have ought against any: that your Father also which is in heaven may forgive you your trespasses. But if ye do not forgive, neither will your Father which is in heaven forgive your trespasses.

MARK 11:25–26

The discretion of a man deferreth his anger; and it is his glory to pass over a transgression.

PROVERBS 19:11

But I say unto you, That ye resist not evil: but whosoever shall smite thee on thy right cheek, turn to him the other also. And if any man will sue thee at the law, and take away thy coat, let him have thy cloak also. And whosoever shall compel thee to go a mile, go with him twain.

MATTHEW 5:39–41

If my people, which are called by my name, shall humble themselves, and pray, and seek my face, and turn from their wicked ways; then will I hear from heaven, and will forgive their sin, and will heal their land.

2 CHRONICLES 7:14

For thou, Lord, art good, and ready to forgive; and plenteous in mercy unto all them that call upon thee.

PSALM 86:5

Judge not, and ye shall not be judged: condemn not, and ye shall not be condemned: forgive, and ye shall be forgiven.

LUKE 6:37

And said unto Simon, Seest thou this woman? . . .she hath washed my feet with tears, and wiped them with the hairs of her head. . .[and] hath not ceased to kiss my feet. . . . This woman hath anointed my feet with ointment. Wherefore I say unto thee, Her sins, which are many, are forgiven; for she loved much: but to whom little is forgiven, the same loveth little. He said unto her, Thy sins are forgiven.

LUKE 7:44–48

Dear God,
forgive me for sinning against You. It hurts me to know that I've failed You, the One who has given me the gift of new life. When others wound me, may I extend to them the same forgiveness that You grant to me. Amen.

Friendship

My friends are my estate.
EMILY DICKINSON

Iron sharpeneth iron; so a man sharpeneth the countenance of his friend.

PROVERBS 27:17

Which of you shall have a friend, and shall go unto him at midnight, and say unto him, Friend, lend me three loaves; for a friend of mine in his journey is come to me, and I have nothing to set before him? And he from within shall answer and say. . .I cannot rise and give thee. I say unto you, Though he will not rise and give him, because he is his friend, yet because of his importunity he will rise and give him as many as he needeth.

LUKE 11:5–8

A friend loveth at all times.

PROVERBS 17:17

A man that hath friends must shew himself friendly: and there is a friend that sticketh closer than a brother.

PROVERBS 18:24

To him that is afflicted pity should be shewed from his friend; but he forsaketh the fear of the Almighty.

JOB 6:14

Faithful are the wounds of a friend.

PROVERBS 27:6

Whosoever therefore will be a friend of the world is the enemy of God.

JAMES 4:4

Heavenly Father,
I praise You for the friends You've provided for me.
Bless them for their investment in my life. Amen.

Generosity

It's not how much we give but how much love we put into giving.
MOTHER TERESA

He hath dispersed, he hath given to the poor; his righteousness endureth for ever; his horn shall be exalted with honour.

PSALM 112:9

Charge them that are rich in this world, that they be not highminded, nor trust in uncertain riches, but in the living God, who giveth us richly all things to enjoy; that they do good, that they be rich in good works, ready to distribute, willing to communicate.

1 TIMOTHY 6:17–18

But when thou makest a feast, call the poor, the maimed, the lame, the blind: and thou shalt be blessed; for they cannot recompense thee: for thou shalt be recompensed at the resurrection of the just.

LUKE 14:13–14

Withhold not good from them to whom it is due, when it is in the power of thine hand to do it. Say not unto thy neighbour, Go, and come again, and to morrow I will give; when thou hast it by thee.

PROVERBS 3:27–28

Therefore when thou doest thine alms, do not sound a trumpet before thee, as the hypocrites do in the synagogues and in the streets, that they may have glory of men. Verily I say unto you, They have their reward. But when thou doest alms, let not thy left hand know what thy right hand doeth: That thine alms may be in secret: and thy Father which seeth in secret himself shall reward thee openly.

MATTHEW 6:2–4

And if thy brother be waxen poor, and fallen in decay with thee; then thou shalt relieve him: yea, though he be a stranger, or a sojourner; that he may live with thee.

LEVITICUS 25:35

If any man or woman that believeth have widows, let them relieve them, and let not the church be charged; that it may relieve them that are widows indeed.

1 TIMOTHY 5:16

And he saw also a certain poor widow casting in thither two mites. And he said, Of a truth I say unto you, that this poor widow hath cast in more than they all: for all these have of their abundance cast in unto the offerings of God: but she of her penury hath cast in all the living that she had.

LUKE 21:2–4

He answereth and saith unto them, He that hath two coats, let him impart to him that hath none; and he that hath meat, let him do likewise.

LUKE 3:11

For the poor shall never cease out of the land: therefore I command thee, saying, Thou shalt open thine hand wide unto thy brother, to thy poor, and to thy needy, in thy land.

DEUTERONOMY 15:11

Every man shall give as he is able, according to the blessing of the LORD thy God which he hath given thee.

DEUTERONOMY 16:17

If a brother or sister be naked, and destitute of daily food, and one of you say unto them, Depart in peace, be ye warmed and filled; notwithstanding ye give them not those things which are needful to the body; what doth it profit?

JAMES 2:15–16

Every man according as he purposeth in his heart, so let him give; not grudgingly, or of necessity: for God loveth a cheerful giver.

2 CORINTHIANS 9:7

Is it not to deal thy bread to the hungry, and that thou bring the poor that are cast out to thy house? when thou seest the naked, that thou cover him; and that thou hide not thyself from thine own flesh? Then shall thy light break forth as the morning, and thine health shall spring forth speedily: and thy righteousness shall go before thee; the glory of the LORD shall be thy rereward.

ISAIAH 58:7–8

For whosoever shall give you a cup of water to drink in my name, because ye belong to Christ, verily I say unto you, he shall not lose his reward.

MARK 9:41

He that despiseth his neighbour sinneth: but he that hath mercy on the poor, happy is he.

PROVERBS 14:21

Give, and it shall be given unto you; good measure, pressed down, and shaken together, and running over, shall men give into your bosom. For with the same measure that ye mete withal it shall be measured to you again.

LUKE 6:38

For ye know the grace of our Lord Jesus Christ, that, though he was rich, yet for your sakes he became poor, that ye through his poverty might be rich.

2 CORINTHIANS 8:9

I have shewed you all things, how that so labouring ye ought to support the weak, and to remember the words of the Lord Jesus, how he said, It is more blessed to give than to receive.

ACTS 20:35

Father,
I want to share all of the blessings You've given to me with others. Loosen my grip when I grasp them too tightly. I will experience joy when I share what I have with others. Amen.

Gentleness

*Take my heart and make it Your dwelling place
so that everyone I touch will be touched also by You!*
ALICE JOYCE DAVIDSON

Put them in mind to be subject to principalities and powers, to obey magistrates, to be ready to every good work, to speak evil of no man, to be no brawlers, but gentle, shewing all meekness unto all men.

TITUS 3:1–2

Take my yoke upon you, and learn of me; for I am meek and lowly in heart: and ye shall find rest unto your souls.

MATTHEW 11:29

But the meek shall inherit the earth; and shall delight themselves in the abundance of peace.

PSALM 37:11

Now I Paul myself beseech you by the meekness and gentleness of Christ, who in presence am base among you, but being absent am bold toward you.

2 CORINTHIANS 10:1

And the servant of the Lord must not strive; but be gentle unto all men, apt to teach, patient, in meekness instructing those that oppose themselves; if God peradventure will give them repentance to the acknowledging of the truth; and that they may recover themselves out of the snare of the devil, who are taken captive by him at his will.

2 TIMOTHY 2:24–26

He shall feed his flock like a shepherd: he shall gather the lambs with his arm, and carry them in his bosom, and shall gently lead those that are with young.

ISAIAH 40:11

The meek will he guide in judgment: and the meek will he teach his way.

PSALM 25:9

But the fruit of the Spirit is love, joy, peace, longsuffering, gentleness, goodness, faith.

GALATIANS 5:22

The meek shall eat and be satisfied: they shall praise the LORD that seek him: your heart shall live for ever.

PSALM 22:26

For the LORD taketh pleasure in his people: he will beautify the meek with salvation.

PSALM 149:4

But the wisdom that is from above is first pure, then peaceable, gentle, and easy to be intreated, full of mercy and good fruits, without partiality, and without hypocrisy.

JAMES 3:17

But we were gentle among you, even as a nurse cherisheth her children: so being affectionately desirous of you, we were willing to have imparted unto you, not the gospel of God only, but also our own souls.

1 THESSALONIANS 2:7

Thou hast also given me the shield of thy salvation: and thy gentleness hath made me great.

2 SAMUEL 22:36

The LORD lifteth up the meek: he casteth the wicked down to the ground.

PSALM 147:6

Sometimes

when life gets overwhelming, I lose patience, Father. Help me to react with a gentle spirit. When I choose gentleness, my circumstances and attitude improve. Ripen the fruit of gentleness in my life. Amen

God's Love

Love has its source in God,
for love is the very essence of His being.
KAY ARTHUR

Behold, what manner of love the Father hath bestowed upon us, that we should be called the sons of God.

1 JOHN 3:1

In this was manifested the love of God toward us, because that God sent his only begotten Son into the world, that we might live through him.

1 JOHN 4:9

I will heal their backsliding, I will love them freely; for mine anger is turned away from him.

HOSEA 14:4

But as it is written, Eye hath not seen, nor ear heard, neither have entered into the heart of man, the things which God hath prepared for them that love him.

1 CORINTHIANS 2:9

For I am persuaded, that neither death, nor life, nor angels, nor principalities, nor powers, nor things present, nor things to come, nor height, nor depth, nor any other creature, shall be able to separate us from the love of God, which is in Christ Jesus our Lord.

ROMANS 8:38–39

The LORD preserveth all them that love him.

PSALM 145:20

And hope maketh not ashamed; because the love of God is shed abroad in our hearts by the Holy Ghost which is given unto us.

ROMANS 5:5

And we have known and believed the love that God hath to us. God is love; and he that dwelleth in love dwelleth in God, and God in him.

1 JOHN 4:16

Herein is love, not that we loved God, but that he loved us, and sent his Son to be the propitiation for our sins.

1 JOHN 4:10

For God so loved the world, that he gave his only begotten Son, that whosoever believeth in him should not perish, but have everlasting life.

JOHN 3:16

But God commendeth his love toward us, in that, while we were yet sinners, Christ died for us.

ROMANS 5:8

For the Father himself loveth you, because ye have loved me, and have believed that I came out from God.

JOHN 16:27

Lord,
*at times when I feel unlovable, thank You
for encompassing me with Your love. Amen.*

God's Provision

*Lift up your eyes. Your heavenly Father waits
to bless you in inconceivable ways to make
your life what you never dreamed it could be.*
ANNE ORTLUND

Therefore I say unto you, Take no thought for your life, what ye
shall eat, or what ye shall drink; nor yet for your body, what ye
shall put on. Is not the life more than meat, and the body than
raiment? Behold the fowls of the air: for they sow not, neither
do they reap, nor gather into barns; yet your heavenly Father
feedeth them. Are ye not much better than they? Which of you
by taking thought can add one cubit unto his stature? And why
take ye thought for raiment? Consider the lilies of the field, how
they grow; they toil not, neither do they spin: And yet I say unto
you, That even Solomon in all his glory was not arrayed like
one of these. Wherefore, if God so clothe the grass of the field,
which to day is, and to morrow is cast into the oven, shall he not
much more clothe you, O ye of little faith? Therefore take no
thought, saying, What shall we eat? or, What shall we drink? or,
Wherewithal shall we be clothed? (For after all these things do the
Gentiles seek:) for your heavenly Father knoweth that ye have need
of all these things. But seek ye first the kingdom of God, and his
righteousness; and all these things shall be added unto you.
MATTHEW 6:25–33

The young lions do lack, and suffer hunger: but they that seek
the LORD shall not want any good thing.

PSALM 34:10

But my God shall supply all your need according to his riches in glory by Christ Jesus.

PHILIPPIANS 4:19

He hath given meat unto them that fear him.

PSALM 111:5

Charge them that are rich in this world, that they be not highminded, nor trust in uncertain riches, but in the living God, who giveth us richly all things to enjoy.

1 TIMOTHY 6:17

God,
*You have given me all that I need to get through this day.
I trust You to provide what I'll need tomorrow. Please help
me to refrain from becoming envious of others' possessions,
and to trust that You will meet my needs. Amen.*

Gratitude

*Simple gratitude helps us experience God
at work in every moment of every day.*
HARRIET CROSBY

And he took the cup, and gave thanks, and gave it to them,
saying, Drink ye all of it.

MATTHEW 26:27

I will praise thee, O LORD, with my whole heart; I will shew
forth all thy marvellous works. I will be glad and rejoice in
thee: I will sing praise to thy name, O thou most High.

PSALM 9:1–2

Blessed be the LORD, that hath given rest unto his people Israel,
according to all that he promised: there hath not failed one word
of all his good promise, which he promised by the hand of Moses
his servant.

1 KINGS 8:56

O LORD, thou hast brought up my soul from the grave: thou
hast kept me alive, that I should not go down to the pit.

PSALM 30:3

He that regardeth the day, regardeth it unto the Lord; and he
that regardeth not the day, to the Lord he doth not regard it. He
that eateth, eateth to the Lord, for he giveth God thanks; and
he that eateth not, to the Lord he eateth not, and giveth God
thanks.

ROMANS 14:6

That I may publish with the voice of thanksgiving, and tell of all thy wondrous works.

PSALM 26:7

Thou hast turned for me my mourning into dancing: thou hast put off my sackcloth, and girded me with gladness; to the end that my glory may sing praise to thee, and not be silent. O LORD my God, I will give thanks unto thee for ever.

PSALM 30:11–12

Giving thanks always for all things unto God and the Father in the name of our Lord Jesus Christ.

EPHESIANS 5:20

And they, continuing daily with one accord in the temple, and breaking bread from house to house, did eat their meat with gladness and singleness of heart, praising God, and having favour with all the people. And the Lord added to the church daily such as should be saved.

ACTS 2:46–47

Many, O LORD my God, are thy wonderful works which thou hast done, and thy thoughts which are to us-ward: they cannot be reckoned up in order unto thee: if I would declare and speak of them, they are more than can be numbered.

PSALM 40:5

I will mention the lovingkindnesses of the LORD, and the praises of the LORD, according to all that the LORD hath bestowed on us, and the great goodness toward the house of Israel, which he hath bestowed on them according to his mercies, and according to the multitude of his lovingkindnesses.

ISAIAH 63:7

I thank thee, and praise thee, O thou God of my fathers, who hast given me wisdom and might, and hast made known unto me now what we desired of thee: for thou hast now made known unto us the king's matter.

DANIEL 2:23

Blessed be the Lord, who daily loadeth us with benefits, even the God of our salvation. Selah.

PSALM 68:19

In every thing give thanks: for this is the will of God in Christ Jesus concerning you.

1 THESSALONIANS 5:18

O give thanks unto the LORD; for he is good: for his mercy endureth for ever.

PSALM 136:1

And he took the seven loaves and the fishes, and gave thanks, and brake them, and gave to his disciples, and the disciples to the multitude.

MATTHEW 15:36

It is a good thing to give thanks unto the LORD, and to sing praises unto thy name, O most High: to shew forth thy lovingkindness in the morning, and thy faithfulness every night.

PSALM 92:1–2

Forgive me
*for the times I'm ungrateful, Lord. I don't intend to
take Your love and blessings for granted. Teach me
to express my thanks—to You and to others. Amen.*

Honesty

Do not do what you would undo if caught.
LEAH ARENDT

Finally, brethren, whatsoever things are true, whatsoever things
are honest, whatsoever things are just, whatsoever things are
pure, whatsoever things are lovely, whatsoever things are of good
report; if there be any virtue, and if there be any praise, think on
these things.

PHILIPPIANS 4:8

Servants, obey in all things your masters according to the flesh;
not with eyeservice, as menpleasers; but in singleness of heart,
fearing God.

COLOSSIANS 3:22

Ye shall not steal, neither deal falsely, neither lie one to another.
LEVITICUS 19:11

The night is far spent, the day is at hand: let us therefore cast off
the works of darkness, and let us put on the armour of light. Let
us walk honestly, as in the day; not in rioting and drunkenness,
not in chambering and wantonness, not in strife and envying.

ROMANS 13:12–13

That ye study to be quiet, and to do your own business, and
to work with your own hands. . . . That ye may walk honestly
toward them that are without, and that ye may have lack of
nothing.

1 THESSALONIANS 4:11–12

Pray for us: for we trust we have a good conscience, in all things willing to live honestly.

HEBREWS 13:18

Be of the same mind one toward another. . . . Recompense to no man evil for evil. Provide things honest in the sight of all men.

ROMANS 12:16–17

Lie not one to another, seeing that ye have put off the old man with his deeds; and have put on the new man, which is renewed in knowledge after the image of him that created him.

COLOSSIANS 3:9–10

He that putteth not out his money to usury, nor taketh reward against the innocent. He that doeth these things shall never be moved.

PSALM 15:5

Providing for honest things, not only in the sight of the Lord, but also in the sight of men.

2 CORINTHIANS 8:21

And herein do I exercise myself, to have always a conscience void of offence toward God, and toward men.

ACTS 24:16

He that walketh righteously, and speaketh uprightly; he that despiseth the gain of oppressions, that shaketh his hands from holding of bribes, that stoppeth his ears from hearing of blood, and shutteth his eyes from seeing evil; he shall dwell on high: his place of defence shall be the munitions of rocks: bread shall be given him; his waters shall be sure.

ISAIAH 33:15–16

Thou knowest the commandments, Do not commit adultery, Do not kill, Do not steal, Do not bear false witness, Defraud not, Honour thy father and mother.

MARK 10:19

Therefore all things whatsoever ye would that men should do to you, do ye even so to them: for this is the law and the prophets.

MATTHEW 7:12

And as ye would that men should do to you, do ye also to them likewise.

LUKE 6:31

Then came also publicans to be baptized, and said unto him, Master, what shall we do? And he said unto them, Exact no more than that which is appointed you.

LUKE 3:12–13

Receive us; we have wronged no man, we have corrupted no man, we have defrauded no man.

2 CORINTHIANS 7:2

My righteousness I hold fast, and will not let it go: my heart shall not reproach me so long as I live.

JOB 27:6

Heavenly Father,
*it seems that it's becoming increasingly acceptable to speak
"partial truths," especially to avoid offending others.
But anything less than complete honesty offends You.
Help me to be a woman of honesty. Amen.*

Hope

Optimism is the faith that leads to achievement.
Nothing can be done without hope and confidence.
HELEN KELLER

Beloved, now are we the sons of God, and it doth not yet appear what we shall be: but we know that, when he shall appear, we shall be like him; for we shall see him as he is. And every man that hath this hope in him purifieth himself, even as he is pure.

1 JOHN 3:2–3

And not only so, but we glory in tribulations also: knowing that tribulation worketh patience; and patience, experience; and experience, hope: and hope maketh not ashamed.

ROMANS 5:3–5

Blessed be the God and Father of our Lord Jesus Christ, which according to his abundant mercy hath begotten us again unto a lively hope by the resurrection of Jesus Christ from the dead.

1 PETER 1:3

The hope of the righteous shall be gladness: but the expectation of the wicked shall perish.

PROVERBS 10:28

But I would not have you to be ignorant, brethren, concerning them which are asleep, that ye sorrow not, even as others which have no hope. For if we believe that Jesus died and rose again, even so them also which sleep in Jesus will God bring with him.

1 THESSALONIANS 4:13–14

Thou art my hiding place and my shield: I hope in thy word.

PSALM 119:114

The LORD is my portion, saith my soul; therefore will I hope in him. The LORD is good unto them that wait for him, to the soul that seeketh him. It is good that a man should both hope and quietly wait for the salvation of the LORD.

LAMENTATIONS 3:24–26

My soul fainteth for thy salvation: but I hope in thy word.

PSALM 119:81

But let us, who are of the day, be sober, putting on the breastplate of faith and love; and for an helmet, the hope of salvation.

1 THESSALONIANS 5:8

But sanctify the Lord God in your hearts: and be ready always to give an answer to every man that asketh you a reason of the hope that is in you with meekness and fear.

1 PETER 3:15

Blessed is the man that trusteth in the LORD, and whose hope the LORD is.

JEREMIAH 17:7

In hope of eternal life, which God, that cannot lie, promised before the world began.

TITUS 1:2

For we through the Spirit wait for the hope of righteousness by faith.

GALATIANS 5:5

But Christ as a son over his own house; whose house are we, if we hold fast the confidence and the rejoicing of the hope firm unto the end.

HEBREWS 3:6

That by two immutable things, in which it was impossible for God to lie, we might have a strong consolation, who have fled for refuge to lay hold upon the hope set before us: which hope we have as an anchor of the soul, both sure and stedfast, and which entereth into that within the veil.

HEBREWS 6:18–19

Now the God of hope fill you with all joy and peace in believing, that ye may abound in hope, through the power of the Holy Ghost.

ROMANS 15:13

To whom God would make known what is the riches of the glory of this mystery among the Gentiles; which is Christ in you, the hope of glory.

COLOSSIANS 1:27

Who by him do believe in God, that raised him up from the dead, and gave him glory; that your faith and hope might be in God.

1 PETER 1:21

And have hope toward God, which they themselves also allow, that there shall be a resurrection of the dead, both of the just and unjust.

ACTS 24:15

And we desire that every one of you do shew the same diligence to the full assurance of hope unto the end.

HEBREWS 6:11

But I will hope continually, and will yet praise thee more and more.

PSALM 71:14

Who against hope believed in hope, that he might become the father of many nations, according to that which was spoken, So shall thy seed be.

ROMANS 4:18

There is one body, and one Spirit, even as ye are called in one hope of your calling.

EPHESIANS 4:4

For we are saved by hope: but hope that is seen is not hope: for what a man seeth, why doth he yet hope for? But if we hope for that we see not, then do we with patience wait for it.

ROMANS 8:24–25

LORD, I have hoped for thy salvation, and done thy commandments.

PSALM 119:166

The eyes of your understanding being enlightened; that ye may know what is the hope of his calling, and what the riches of the glory of his inheritance in the saints.

EPHESIANS 1:18

According to my earnest expectation and my hope, that in nothing I shall be ashamed, but that with all boldness, as always, so now also Christ shall be magnified in my body, whether it be by life, or by death.

PHILIPPIANS 1:20

Seeing then that we have such hope, we use great plainness of speech.

2 CORINTHIANS 3:12

Remember the word unto thy servant, upon which thou hast caused me to hope.

PSALM 119:49

Why art thou cast down, O my soul? and why art thou disquieted within me? hope thou in God: for I shall yet praise him, who is the health of my countenance, and my God.

PSALM 42:11

For the hope which is laid up for you in heaven, whereof ye heard before in the word of the truth of the gospel.

COLOSSIANS 1:5

Looking for that blessed hope, and the glorious appearing of the great God and our Saviour Jesus Christ.

TITUS 2:13

Now faith is the substance of things hoped for, the evidence of things not seen.

HEBREWS 11:1

For the needy shall not alway be forgotten: the expectation of the poor shall not perish for ever.

PSALM 9:18

What a joy
*to hope in You, Jesus. I know that all of Your promises are true,
and I anticipate praising You in heaven throughout eternity.
Amen.*

Hospitality

*Just allow your guest to feel at ease because you are,
whatever the state of your house. This is an
important element to being a gracious host.*
LINDA DAVIS ZUMBEHL

Be not forgetful to entertain strangers: for thereby some have
entertained angels unawares.

HEBREWS 13:2

Use hospitality one to another without grudging.

1 PETER 4:9

And if a stranger sojourn with thee in your land, ye shall not vex
him. But the stranger that dwelleth with you shall be unto you as
one born among you, and thou shalt love him as thyself.

LEVITICUS 19:33–34

Be blameless, as the steward of God; not selfwilled, not soon angry,
not given to wine, no striker, not given to filthy lucre; but a lover
of hospitality, a lover of good men, sober, just, holy, temperate.

TITUS 1:7–8

Wisdom hath builded her house, she hath hewn out her seven
pillars: she hath killed her beasts; she hath mingled her wine; she
hath also furnished her table. She hath sent forth her maidens:
she crieth upon the highest places of the city, whoso is simple, let
him turn in hither: as for him that wanteth understanding, she
saith to him, come, eat of my bread, and drink of the wine which
I have mingled.

PROVERBS 9:1–5

Distributing to the necessity of saints; given to hospitality.

ROMANS 12:13

Then shall the King say unto them on his right hand, Come, ye blessed of my Father, inherit the kingdom prepared for you from the foundation of the world: for I was an hungred, and ye gave me meat: I was thirsty, and ye gave me drink: I was a stranger, and ye took me in: naked, and ye clothed me: I was sick, and ye visited me: I was in prison, and ye came unto me. . . . And the King shall answer and say unto them, Verily I say unto you, Inasmuch as ye have done it unto one of the least of these my brethren, ye have done it unto me.

MATTHEW 25:34–36, 40

But when thou makest a feast, call the poor, the maimed, the lame, the blind: and thou shalt be blessed; for they cannot recompense thee: for thou shalt be recompensed at the resurrection of the just.

LUKE 14:13–14

Well reported of for good works; if she have brought up children, if she have lodged strangers, if she have washed the saints' feet, if she have relieved the afflicted, if she have diligently followed every good work.

1 TIMOTHY 5:10

And thou shalt not glean thy vineyard, neither shalt thou gather every grape of thy vineyard; thou shalt leave them for the poor and stranger: I am the LORD your God.

LEVITICUS 19:10

If a brother or sister be naked, and destitute of daily food, and one of you say unto them, Depart in peace, be ye warmed and filled; notwithstanding ye give them not those things which are needful to the body; what doth it profit?

JAMES 2:15–16

He doth execute the judgment of the fatherless and widow, and loveth the stranger, in giving him food and raiment.

DEUTERONOMY 10:18

For whosoever shall give you a cup of water to drink in my name, because ye belong to Christ, verily I say unto you, he shall not lose his reward.

MARK 9:41

Dear Lord,
*I give my home to You. Please fill it with love and laughter.
Help me to keep it in order, so that I can be prepared
to host both friends and strangers. Amen.*

Joy

Laughter lightens the load.
PATSY CLAIRMONT

And the angel said unto them, Fear not: for, behold, I bring you good tidings of great joy, which shall be to all people.

LUKE 2:10

Rejoice in the LORD always: and again I say, Rejoice.

PHILIPPIANS 4:4

The LORD is my strength and my shield; my heart trusted in him, and I am helped: therefore my heart greatly rejoiceth; and with my song will I praise him.

PSALM 28:7

Hitherto have ye asked nothing in my name: ask, and ye shall receive, that your joy may be full.

JOHN 16:24

Be glad in the LORD, and rejoice, ye righteous: and shout for joy, all ye that are upright in heart.

PSALM 32:11

In the transgression of an evil man there is a snare: but the righteous doth sing and rejoice.

PROVERBS 29:6

As sorrowful, yet alway rejoicing; as poor, yet making many rich; as having nothing, and yet possessing all things.

2 CORINTHIANS 6:10

My lips shall greatly rejoice when I sing unto thee; and my soul, which thou hast redeemed.

PSALM 71:23

Therefore the redeemed of the LORD shall return, and come with singing unto Zion; and everlasting joy shall be upon their head: they shall obtain gladness and joy; and sorrow and mourning shall flee away.

ISAIAH 51:11

A merry heart doeth good like a medicine.

PROVERBS 17:22

Make a joyful noise unto the LORD, all ye lands. Serve the LORD with gladness: come before his presence with singing.

PSALM 100:1–2

His lord said unto him, Well done, thou good and faithful servant: thou hast been faithful over a few things, I will make thee ruler over many things: enter thou into the joy of thy lord.

MATTHEW 25:21

Rejoice ye in that day, and leap for joy: for, behold, your reward is great in heaven: for in the like manner did their fathers unto the prophets.

LUKE 6:23

And now come I to thee; and these things I speak in the world, that they might have my joy fulfilled in themselves.

JOHN 17:13

All the days of the afflicted are evil: but he that is of a merry heart hath a continual feast.

PROVERBS 15:15

Let all those that seek thee rejoice and be glad in thee: let such as love thy salvation say continually, The LORD be magnified.

PSALM 40:16

And not only so, but we also joy in God through our Lord Jesus Christ, by whom we have now received the atonement.

ROMANS 5:11

Not for that we have dominion over your faith, but are helpers of your joy: for by faith ye stand.

2 CORINTHIANS 1:24

For our heart shall rejoice in him, because we have trusted in his holy name.

PSALM 33:21

Speaking to yourselves in psalms and hymns and spiritual songs, singing and making melody in your heart to the Lord.

EPHESIANS 5:19

Is any merry? let him sing psalms.

JAMES 5:13

I will greatly rejoice in the LORD, my soul shall be joyful in my God; for he hath clothed me with the garments of salvation, he hath covered me with the robe of righteousness, as a bridegroom decketh himself with ornaments, and as a bride adorneth herself with her jewels.

ISAIAH 61:10

Lord,
allow me to see the humor in life. Please don't let me take life too seriously. Remind me to share my happiness with others—my smile may be the only one another person receives today. Amen.

Kindness

Let no one ever come to you without leaving better and happier.
Be the living expression of God's kindness: kindness in your face,
kindness in your eyes, kindness in your smile.
MOTHER TERESA

Give to every man that asketh of thee; and of him that taketh
away thy goods ask them not again.

LUKE 6:30

Not rendering evil for evil, or railing for railing: but contrariwise
blessing; knowing that ye are thereunto called, that ye should
inherit a blessing.

1 PETER 3:9

She openeth her mouth with wisdom; and in her tongue is the
law of kindness.

PROVERBS 31:26

Put on therefore, as the elect of God, holy and beloved, bowels of
mercies, kindness, humbleness of mind, meekness, longsuffering.
COLOSSIANS 3:12

And if ye lend to them of whom ye hope to receive, what thank
have ye? for sinners also lend to sinners, to receive as much again.
But love ye your enemies, and do good, and lend, hoping for
nothing again; and your reward shall be great, and ye shall be the
children of the Highest: for he is kind unto the unthankful and
to the evil.

LUKE 6:34–35

And to godliness brotherly kindness; and to brotherly kindness charity. For if these things be in you, and abound. . .ye shall neither be barren nor unfruitful in the knowledge of our Lord Jesus Christ.

2 PETER 1:7–8

As we have therefore opportunity, let us do good unto all men, especially unto them who are of the household of faith.

GALATIANS 6:10

Thus speaketh the LORD of hosts, saying, Execute true judgment, and shew mercy and compassions every man to his brother. And oppress not the widow, nor the fatherless, the stranger, nor the poor; and let none of you imagine evil against his brother in your heart.

ZECHARIAH 7:9–10

Let every one of us please his neighbour for his good to edification.

ROMANS 15:2

He that despiseth his neighbour sinneth: but he that hath mercy on the poor, happy is he.

PROVERBS 14:21

Give to him that asketh thee, and from him that would borrow of thee turn not thou away.

MATTHEW 5:42

Who can have compassion on the ignorant, and on them that are out of the way; for that he himself also is compassed with infirmity.

HEBREWS 5:2

And he said, Blessed be thou of the LORD, my daughter: for thou hast shewed more kindness in the latter end than at the beginning. . . . And now, my daughter, fear not; I will do to thee all that thou requirest.

RUTH 3:10–11

Rejoice with them that do rejoice, and weep with them that weep.

ROMANS 12:15

The desire of a man is his kindness: and a poor man is better than a liar. The fear of the LORD tendeth to life: and he that hath it shall abide satisfied.

PROVERBS 19:22–23

But in all things approving ourselves as the ministers of God. . .by pureness, by knowledge, by longsuffering, by kindness. . .as having nothing, and yet possessing all things.

2 CORINTHIANS 6:4, 6, 10

Heavenly Father,
please help me to be kind to those around me today. Change my thoughts. Control my tongue. Let them see Your love through me. Amen.

Love for Others

*If I put my own good name before the other's highest good,
then I know nothing of Calvary love.*
AMY CARMICHAEL

Be kindly affectioned one to another with brotherly love; in
honour preferring one another.

ROMANS 12:10

But as touching brotherly love ye need not that I write unto
you: for ye yourselves are taught of God to love one another.

1 THESSALONIANS 4:9

For all the law is fulfilled in one word, even in this; Thou shalt
love thy neighbour as thyself.

GALATIANS 5:14

He that loveth not knoweth not God; for God is love.

1 JOHN 4:8

And to godliness brotherly kindness; and to brotherly kindness
charity.

2 PETER 1:7

Beloved, if God so loved us, we ought also to love one another.
No man hath seen God at any time. If we love one another,
God dwelleth in us, and his love is perfected in us.

1 JOHN 4:11–12

And now abideth faith, hope, charity, these three; but the greatest of these is charity.

1 Corinthians 13:13

Ye have heard that it hath been said, Thou shalt love thy neighbour, and hate thine enemy. But I say unto you, Love your enemies, bless them that curse you, do good to them that hate you, and pray for them which despitefully use you, and persecute you; that ye may be the children of your Father which is in heaven: for he maketh his sun to rise on the evil and on the good, and sendeth rain on the just and on the unjust.

Matthew 5:43–45

For this is the message that ye heard from the beginning, that we should love one another.

1 John 3:11

Thou shalt not avenge, nor bear any grudge against the children of thy people, but thou shalt love thy neighbour as thyself: I am the Lord.

Leviticus 19:18

Though I speak with the tongues of men and of angels, and have not charity, I am become as sounding brass, or a tinkling cymbal. And though I have the gift of prophecy, and understand all mysteries, and all knowledge; and though I have all faith, so that I could remove mountains, and have not charity, I am nothing. And though I bestow all my goods to feed the poor, and though I give my body to be burned, and have not charity, it profiteth me nothing.

1 Corinthians 13:1–3

Owe no man any thing, but to love one another: for he that loveth another hath fulfilled the law.

ROMANS 13:8

And let us consider one another to provoke unto love and to good works.

HEBREWS 10:24

In this the children of God are manifest, and the children of the devil: whosoever doeth not righteousness is not of God, neither he that loveth not his brother.

1 JOHN 3:10

And through thy knowledge shall the weak brother perish, for whom Christ died? But when ye sin so against the brethren, and wound their weak conscience, ye sin against Christ.

1 CORINTHIANS 8:11–12

This is my commandment, That ye love one another, as I have loved you. Greater love hath no man than this, that a man lay down his life for his friends.

JOHN 15:12–13

I speak to your shame. Is it so, that there is not a wise man among you? no, not one that shall be able to judge between his brethren? But brother goeth to law with brother, and that before the unbelievers. Now therefore there is utterly a fault among you, because ye go to law one with another. Why do ye not rather take wrong? why do ye not rather suffer yourselves to be defrauded? Nay, ye do wrong, and defraud, and that your brethren.

1 CORINTHIANS 6:5–8

For, brethren, ye have been called unto liberty; only use not liberty for an occasion to the flesh, but by love serve one another. For all the law is fulfilled in one word, even in this; Thou shalt love thy neighbour as thyself.

GALATIANS 5:13–14

If a man say, I love God, and hateth his brother, he is a liar: for he that loveth not his brother whom he hath seen, how can he love God whom he hath not seen? And this commandment have we from him, That he who loveth God love his brother also.

1 JOHN 4:20–21

Leave there thy gift before the altar, and go thy way; first be reconciled to thy brother, and then come and offer thy gift.

MATTHEW 5:24

Seeing ye have purified your souls in obeying the truth through the Spirit unto unfeigned love of the brethren, see that ye love one another with a pure heart fervently.

1 PETER 1:22

Beloved, let us love one another: for love is of God; and every one that loveth is born of God, and knoweth God. . . . In this was manifested the love of God toward us, because that God sent his only begotten Son into the world, that we might live through him. Herein is love, not that we loved God, but that he loved us, and sent his Son to be the propitiation for our sins. Beloved, if God so loved us, we ought also to love one another.

1 JOHN 4:7, 9-11

Honour all men. Love the brotherhood. Fear God. Honour the king.

1 PETER 2:17

A new commandment I give unto you, That ye love one another; as I have loved you, that ye also love one another. By this shall all men know that ye are my disciples, if ye have love one to another.

JOHN 13:34–35

Hereby perceive we the love of God, because he laid down his life for us: and we ought to lay down our lives for the brethren. But whoso hath this world's good, and seeth his brother have need, and shutteth up his bowels of compassion from him, how dwelleth the love of God in him? My little children, let us not love in word, neither in tongue; but in deed and in truth. And hereby we know that we are of the truth, and shall assure our hearts before him.

1 JOHN 3:16–19

Heavenly Father,
*help me to love others unconditionally. As I'm reminded that
You love me in spite of my imperfections, let me extend
that same love to those I come in contact with. Amen.*

Meekness

We can do no great things;
only small things with great love.
MOTHER TERESA

Brethren, if a man be overtaken in a fault, ye which are spiritual, restore such an one in the spirit of meekness; considering thyself, lest thou also be tempted. Bear ye one another's burdens, and so fulfil the law of Christ.

GALATIANS 6:1–2

The meek shall eat and be satisfied: they shall praise the LORD that seek him: your heart shall live for ever.

PSALM 22:26

Great is our Lord, and of great power: his understanding is infinite. The LORD lifteth up the meek: he casteth the wicked down to the ground.

PSALM 147:5–6

The meek also shall increase their joy in the LORD, and the poor among men shall rejoice in the Holy One of Israel.

ISAIAH 29:19

The Spirit of the Lord GOD is upon me; because the LORD hath anointed me to preach good tidings unto the meek; he hath sent me to bind up the brokenhearted, to proclaim liberty to the captives, and the opening of the prison to them that are bound.

ISAIAH 61:1

Blessed are the meek: for they shall inherit the earth.

MATTHEW 5:5

Likewise, ye wives, be in subjection to your own husbands; that, if any obey not the word, they also may without the word be won by the conversation of the wives. . . . Whose adorning let it not be that outward adorning of plaiting the hair, and of wearing of gold, or of putting on of apparel; but let it be the hidden man of the heart, in that which is not corruptible, even the ornament of a meek and quiet spirit, which is in the sight of God of great price.

1 PETER 3:1, 3–4

Seek ye the LORD, all ye meek of the earth, which have wrought his judgment; seek righteousness, seek meekness: it may be ye shall be hid in the day of the LORD's anger.

ZEPHANIAH 2:3

But the meek shall inherit the earth; and shall delight themselves in the abundance of peace.

PSALM 37:11

Good and upright is the LORD: therefore will he teach sinners in the way. The meek will he guide in judgment: and the meek will he teach his way.

PSALM 25:8–9

Lord God,
I pray that I will have a spirit of meekness. Help me to follow Your example, being mild, yet not weak. For if I can maintain this balance, I will have strength through You. Amen.

Mercy

God deals with us from a merciful posture; His arms are open, His words are healing, He wants sinners to return to Him.
MARTIE STOWELL

But thou, O Lord, art a God full of compassion, and gracious, longsuffering, and plenteous in mercy and truth.

PSALM 86:15

Be ye therefore merciful, as your Father also is merciful.

LUKE 6:36

Therefore turn thou to thy God: keep mercy and judgment, and wait on thy God continually.

HOSEA 12:6

Behold, we count them happy which endure. Ye have heard of the patience of Job, and have seen the end of the Lord; that the Lord is very pitiful, and of tender mercy.

JAMES 5:11

For thou, Lord, art good, and ready to forgive; and plenteous in mercy unto all them that call upon thee.

PSALM 86:5

He hath shewed thee, O man, what is good; and what doth the LORD require of thee, but to do justly, and to love mercy, and to walk humbly with thy God?

MICAH 6:8

Blessed are the merciful: for they shall obtain mercy.

MATTHEW 5:7

Thou art a God ready to pardon, gracious and merciful, slow to anger, and of great kindness.

NEHEMIAH 9:17

Blessed be the God and Father of our Lord Jesus Christ, which according to his abundant mercy hath begotten us again unto a lively hope by the resurrection of Jesus Christ from the dead.

1 PETER 1:3

For God hath concluded them all in unbelief, that he might have mercy upon all.

ROMANS 11:32

Let not mercy and truth forsake thee: bind them about thy neck; write them upon the table of thine heart: so shalt thou find favour and good understanding in the sight of God and man.

PROVERBS 3:3–4

The LORD is good to all: and his tender mercies are over all his works.

PSALM 145:9

He that covereth his sins shall not prosper: but whoso confesseth and forsaketh them shall have mercy.

PROVERBS 28:13

But God, who is rich in mercy, for his great love wherewith he loved us, even when we were dead in sins, hath quickened us together with Christ, (by grace ye are saved).

EPHESIANS 2:4–5

Not by works of righteousness which we have done, but according to his mercy he saved us, by the washing of regeneration, and renewing of the Holy Ghost; which he shed on us abundantly through Jesus Christ our Saviour; that being justified by his grace, we should be made heirs according to the hope of eternal life.

TITUS 3:5–7

Let the wicked forsake his way, and the unrighteous man his thoughts: and let him return unto the LORD, and he will have mercy upon him; and to our God, for he will abundantly pardon.

ISAIAH 55:7

For I will be merciful to their unrighteousness, and their sins and their iniquities will I remember no more. In that he saith, A new covenant, he hath made the first old. Now that which decayeth and waxeth old is ready to vanish away.

HEBREWS 8:12–13

And his mercy is on them that fear him from generation to generation.

LUKE 1:50

Mercy and truth are met together; righteousness and peace have kissed each other.

PSALM 85:10

Father,
forgive me for keeping record of wrongs others have committed against me. Just as You have forgotten all of my sins and failures, let me show that same mercy to others. Erase the wrongs from my memory, I pray. Amen.

Modesty

*A woman with a gentle and quiet spirit is not only precious
to God, but she is attractive to others also. She dresses
appropriately, but it is her inner adornment that is noted
because she is secure and at rest within her spirit.*
CYNTHIA HEALD

In like manner also, that women adorn themselves in modest
apparel, with shamefacedness and sobriety; not with broided
hair, or gold, or pearls, or costly array. But (which becometh
women professing godliness) with good works.

1 TIMOTHY 2:9–10

Let no man deceive himself. If any man among you seemeth to be
wise in this world, let him become a fool, that he may be wise.

1 CORINTHIANS 3:18

A man's pride shall bring him low: but honour shall uphold the
humble in spirit.

PROVERBS 29:23

Let another man praise thee, and not thine own mouth;
a stranger, and not thine own lips.

PROVERBS 27:2

The aged women likewise, that they be in behaviour as becometh
holiness, not false accusers, not given to much wine, teachers of
good things; that they may teach the young women to be sober, to
love their husbands, to love their children, to be discreet, chaste,
keepers at home, good, obedient to their own husbands, that the
word of God be not blasphemed.

TITUS 2:3–5

But now ye rejoice in your boastings: all such rejoicing is evil.

JAMES 4:16

And base things of the world, and things which are despised, hath God chosen, yea, and things which are not, to bring to nought things that are: that no flesh should glory in his presence.

1 CORINTHIANS 1:28–29

Dear Lord,
I want to demonstrate modesty in my life. I will clothe myself outwardly in a manner that pleases You and will adorn myself inwardly with a gentle spirit. Amen.

Obedience

The only way I will keep a pliable, obedient spirit in the larger decisions is to look to Him and to obey in the smaller ones.
CATHERINE MARSHALL

Now therefore, if ye will obey my voice indeed, and keep my covenant, then ye shall be a peculiar treasure unto me above all people: for all the earth is mine.

EXODUS 19:5

If they obey and serve him, they shall spend their days in prosperity, and their years in pleasures.

JOB 36:11

Thou shalt keep therefore his statutes, and his commandments, which I command thee this day, that it may go well with thee, and with thy children after thee, and that thou mayest prolong thy days upon the earth, which the LORD thy God giveth thee, for ever.

DEUTERONOMY 4:40

My son, forget not my law; but let thine heart keep my commandments: For length of days, and long life, and peace, shall they add to thee.

PROVERBS 3:1–2

Observe and hear all these words which I command thee, that it may go well with thee, and with thy children after thee for ever, when thou doest that which is good and right in the sight of the LORD thy God.

DEUTERONOMY 12:28

But whoso looketh into the perfect law of liberty, and continueth therein, he being not a forgetful hearer, but a doer of the work, this man shall be blessed in his deed.

JAMES 1:25

Those things, which ye have both learned, and received, and heard, and seen in me, do: and the God of peace shall be with you.

PHILIPPIANS 4:9

Not every one that saith unto me, Lord, Lord, shall enter into the kingdom of heaven; but he that doeth the will of my Father which is in heaven.

· MATTHEW 7:21

Let us hear the conclusion of the whole matter: Fear God, and keep his commandments: for this is the whole duty of man.

ECCLESIASTES 12:13

I command thee this day to love the LORD thy God, to walk in his ways, and to keep his commandments and his statutes and his judgments, that thou mayest live and multiply: and the LORD thy God shall bless thee in the land whither thou goest to possess it.

DEUTERONOMY 30:16

If ye keep my commandments, ye shall abide in my love; even as I have kept my Father's commandments, and abide in his love.

JOHN 15:10

And Samuel said, Hath the LORD as great delight in burnt offerings and sacrifices, as in obeying the voice of the LORD? Behold, to obey is better than sacrifice, and to hearken than the fat of rams.

1 SAMUEL 15:22

All the paths of the LORD are mercy and truth unto such as keep his covenant and his testimonies.

PSALM 25:10

Whosoever therefore shall break one of these least commandments, and shall teach men so, he shall be called the least in the kingdom of heaven: but whosoever shall do and teach them, the same shall be called great in the kingdom of heaven.

MATTHEW 5:19

For not the hearers of the law are just before God, but the doers of the law shall be justified.

ROMANS 2:13

And the world passeth away, and the lust thereof: but he that doeth the will of God abideth for ever.

1 JOHN 2:17

But he said, Yea rather, blessed are they that hear the word of God, and keep it.

LUKE 11:28

Keep therefore the words of this covenant, and do them, that ye may prosper in all that ye do.

DEUTERONOMY 29:9

Furthermore we have had fathers of our flesh which corrected us, and we gave them reverence: shall we not much rather be in subjection unto the Father of spirits, and live?

HEBREWS 12:9

If ye be willing and obedient, ye shall eat the good of the land.

ISAIAH 1:19

Blessed are they that keep his testimonies, and that seek him with the whole heart.

PSALM 119:2

Wherefore, my beloved, as ye have always obeyed, not as in my presence only, but now much more in my absence, work out your own salvation with fear and trembling.

PHILIPPIANS 2:12

Father,
the path of life is often difficult. I ask not that You make it smooth,
but to illuminate it so that I can see to walk in obedience. If for
a moment the light is dim, let me walk by faith, trusting You
with each step I take. For Your way is perfect. Amen.

Patience

Obedience is the fruit of faith;
patience, the bloom on the fruit.
CHRISTINA ROSSETTI

And the servant of the Lord must not strive; but be gentle unto all men, apt to teach, patient.

2 TIMOTHY 2:24

For ye have need of patience, that, after ye have done the will of God, ye might receive the promise.

HEBREWS 10:36

Rest in the LORD, and wait patiently for him: fret not thyself because of him who prospereth in his way, because of the man who bringeth wicked devices to pass. Cease from anger, and forsake wrath: fret not thyself in any wise to do evil. For evildoers shall be cut off: but those that wait upon the LORD, they shall inherit the earth.

PSALM 37:7–9

Here is the patience of the saints: here are they that keep the commandments of God, and the faith of Jesus.

REVELATION 14:12

Knowing this, that the trying of your faith worketh patience. But let patience have her perfect work, that ye may be perfect and entire, wanting nothing.

JAMES 1:3–4

But that on the good ground are they, which in an honest and good heart, having heard the word, keep it, and bring forth fruit with patience.

LUKE 8:15

And let us not be weary in well doing: for in due season we shall reap, if we faint not.

GALATIANS 6:9

And not only so, but we glory in tribulations also: knowing that tribulation worketh patience; and patience, experience; and experience, hope.

ROMANS 5:3–4

But in all things approving ourselves as the ministers of God, in much patience, in afflictions, in necessities, in distresses.

2 CORINTHIANS 6:4

Now we exhort you, brethren, warn them that are unruly, comfort the feebleminded, support the weak, be patient toward all men.

1 THESSALONIANS 5:14

For whatsoever things were written aforetime were written for our learning, that we through patience and comfort of the scriptures might have hope. Now the God of patience and consolation grant you to be likeminded one toward another according to Christ Jesus.

ROMANS 15:4–5

And the Lord direct your hearts into the love of God, and into the patient waiting for Christ.

2 THESSALONIANS 3:5

In your patience possess ye your souls.

LUKE 21:19

Wherefore seeing we also are compassed about with so great a cloud of witnesses, let us lay aside every weight, and the sin which doth so easily beset us, and let us run with patience the race that is set before us.

HEBREWS 12:1

To them who by patient continuance in well doing seek for glory and honour and immortality, eternal life.

ROMANS 2:7

Be patient therefore, brethren, unto the coming of the Lord. Behold, the husbandman waiteth for the precious fruit of the earth, and hath long patience for it, until he receive the early and latter rain. Be ye also patient; stablish your hearts: for the coming of the Lord draweth nigh.

JAMES 5:7–8

That ye be not slothful, but followers of them who through faith and patience inherit the promises.

HEBREWS 6:12

For what glory is it, if, when ye be buffeted for your faults, ye shall take it patiently? but if, when ye do well, and suffer for it, ye take it patiently, this is acceptable with God.

1 PETER 2:20

Better is the end of a thing than the beginning thereof: and the patient in spirit is better than the proud in spirit. Be not hasty in thy spirit to be angry: for anger resteth in the bosom of fools.

ECCLESIASTES 7:8–9

And so, after he had patiently endured, he obtained the promise.

Lord,
*sometimes I look for a sign. I want the writing on the wall
or a burning bush experience. I feel like I need direction,
and I need it now! Lord, give me patience. Give me faith.
Instead of seeking a sign, let me live expectantly for the everyday
miracles and listen for Your still, small voice. Amen.*

Peace

*When the presence of the Lord really becomes your experience,
you will actually discover that you have gradually begun to love
this silence and peaceful rest which come with His presence.*
MADAME GUYON

The LORD will give strength unto his people; the LORD will bless
his people with peace.

PSALM 29:11

For the mountains shall depart, and the hills be removed; but my
kindness shall not depart from thee, neither shall the covenant of
my peace be removed, saith the LORD that hath mercy on thee. . . .
And all thy children shall be taught of the LORD; and great shall be
the peace of thy children.

ISAIAH 54:10, 13

Now the God of hope fill you with all joy and peace in believing,
that ye may abound in hope, through the power of the Holy
Ghost.

ROMANS 15:13

When a man's ways please the LORD, he maketh even his enemies
to be at peace with him.

PROVERBS 16:7

Blessed are the peacemakers: for they shall be called the children
of God.

MATTHEW 5:9

Deceit is in the heart of them that imagine evil: but to the counsellors of peace is joy.

PROVERBS 12:20

And the peace of God, which passeth all understanding, shall keep your hearts and minds through Christ Jesus.

PHILIPPIANS 4:7

And the fruit of righteousness is sown in peace of them that make peace.

JAMES 3:18

Endeavouring to keep the unity of the Spirit in the bond of peace.

EPHESIANS 4:3

Glory to God in the highest, and on earth peace, good will toward men.

LUKE 2:14

Flee also youthful lusts: but follow righteousness, faith, charity, peace, with them that call on the Lord out of a pure heart.

2 TIMOTHY 2:22

Mark the perfect man, and behold the upright: for the end of that man is peace.

PSALM 37:37

And he shall judge among the nations, and shall rebuke many people: and they shall beat their swords into plowshares, and their spears into pruninghooks: nation shall not lift up sword against nation, neither shall they learn war any more.

ISAIAH 2:4

If it be possible, as much as lieth in you, live peaceably with all men.

ROMANS 12:18

And to esteem them very highly in love for their work's sake. And be at peace among yourselves.

1 THESSALONIANS 5:13

I exhort therefore, that, first of all, supplications, prayers, intercessions, and giving of thanks, be made for all men; for kings, and for all that are in authority; that we may lead a quiet and peaceable life in all godliness and honesty.

1 TIMOTHY 2:1–2

Follow peace with all men, and holiness, without which no man shall see the Lord.

HEBREWS 12:14

Behold, how good and how pleasant it is for brethren to dwell together in unity!

PSALM 133:1

For he that will love life, and see good days, let him refrain his tongue from evil, and his lips that they speak no guile: let him eschew evil, and do good; let him seek peace, and ensue it.

1 PETER 3:10–11

Thou wilt keep him in perfect peace, whose mind is stayed on thee: because he trusteth in thee.

ISAIAH 26:3

For God hath not given us the spirit of fear; but of power, and of love, and of a sound mind.

2 TIMOTHY 1:7

Peace I leave with you, my peace I give unto you: not as the world giveth, give I unto you. Let not your heart be troubled, neither let it be afraid.

JOHN 14:27

Lord,
I often become distracted with the activities of everyday life. Please give me a calm spirit, and help me to rest in Your perfect peace. Amen.

Perseverance

You may have to fight a battle
more than once to win it.
MARGARET THATCHER

For the which cause I also suffer these things: nevertheless I am not ashamed: for I know whom I have believed, and am persuaded that he is able to keep that which I have committed unto him against that day. Hold fast the form of sound words, which thou hast heard of me, in faith and love which is in Christ Jesus.

2 TIMOTHY 1:12–13

That the trial of your faith, being much more precious than of gold that perisheth, though it be tried with fire, might be found unto praise and honour and glory at the appearing of Jesus Christ.

1 PETER 1:7

He that hath an ear, let him hear what the Spirit saith unto the churches; He that overcometh shall not be hurt of the second death.

REVELATION 2:11

For we are made partakers of Christ, if we hold the beginning of our confidence stedfast unto the end.

HEBREWS 3:14

To him that overcometh will I grant to sit with me in my throne, even as I also overcame, and am set down with my Father in his throne.

REVELATION 3:21

Thou therefore endure hardness, as a good soldier of Jesus Christ.

2 TIMOTHY 2:3

Praying always with all prayer and supplication in the Spirit, and watching thereunto with all perseverance and supplication for all saints.

EPHESIANS 6:18

Teaching us that, denying ungodliness and worldly lusts, we should live soberly, righteously, and godly, in this present world; looking for that blessed hope, and the glorious appearing of the great God and our Saviour Jesus Christ.

TITUS 2:12–13

Though he fall, he shall not be utterly cast down: for the LORD upholdeth him with his hand.

PSALM 37:24

Let us hold fast the profession of our faith without wavering; (for he is faithful that promised).

HEBREWS 10:23

For I am persuaded, that neither death, nor life, nor angels, nor principalities, nor powers, nor things present, nor things to come, nor height, nor depth, nor any other creature, shall be able to separate us from the love of God, which is in Christ Jesus our Lord.

ROMANS 8:38–39

Stand fast therefore in the liberty wherewith Christ hath made us free, and be not entangled again with the yoke of bondage.

GALATIANS 5:1

But the path of the just is as the shining light, that shineth more and more unto the perfect day.

PROVERBS 4:18

Then said Jesus to those Jews which believed on him, If ye continue in my word, then are ye my disciples indeed.

JOHN 8:31

For now we live, if ye stand fast in the Lord.

1 THESSALONIANS 3:8

Ye therefore, beloved, seeing ye know these things before, beware lest ye also, being led away with the error of the wicked, fall from your own stedfastness.

2 PETER 3:17

Confirming the souls of the disciples, and exhorting them to continue in the faith, and that we must through much tribulation enter into the kingdom of God.

ACTS 14:22

Wherefore seeing we also are compassed about with so great a cloud of witnesses, let us lay aside every weight, and the sin which doth so easily beset us, and let us run with patience the race that is set before us, looking unto Jesus the author and finisher of our faith; who for the joy that was set before him endured the cross, despising the shame, and is set down at the right hand of the throne of God.

HEBREWS 12:1–2

Therefore, my brethren dearly beloved and longed for, my joy and crown, so stand fast in the Lord, my dearly beloved.

PHILIPPIANS 4:1

Who shall separate us from the love of Christ? shall tribulation, or distress, or persecution, or famine, or nakedness, or peril, or sword?

ROMANS 8:35

Wherefore take unto you the whole armour of God, that ye may be able to withstand in the evil day, and having done all, to stand.

EPHESIANS 6:13

Father,
sometimes I get so weary and want to give up. But You have
promised a life of blessing if I will persevere. Thank You for
giving me the strength I need to "run the race." Amen.

Power

*The stone still stood there in that quiet garden,
a reminder of the reality of the problem we all must live
with; but Christ had moved it to one side so very easily,
demonstrating His resurrection power on our behalf.*
JILL BRISCOE

Seek the LORD and his strength, seek his face continually.

1 CHRONICLES 16:11

The LORD thy God in the midst of thee is mighty; he will save,
he will rejoice over thee with joy; he will rest in his love, he will
joy over thee with singing.

ZEPHANIAH 3:17

Now unto him that is able to do exceeding abundantly above all
that we ask or think, according to the power that worketh in us.

EPHESIANS 3:20

But ye shall receive power, after that the Holy Ghost is come
upon you: and ye shall be witnesses unto me both in Jerusalem,
and in all Judaea, and in Samaria, and unto the uttermost part of
the earth.

ACTS 1:8

And what is the exceeding greatness of his power to us-ward
who believe, according to the working of his mighty power,
which he wrought in Christ, when he raised him from the dead,
and set him at his own right hand in the heavenly places.

EPHESIANS 1:19–20

For the kingdom of God is not in word, but in power.

1 CORINTHIANS 4:20

For our gospel came not unto you in word only, but also in power, and in the Holy Ghost, and in much assurance; as ye know what manner of men we were among you for your sake.

1 THESSALONIANS 1:5

For though he was crucified through weakness, yet he liveth by the power of God. For we also are weak in him, but we shall live with him by the power of God toward you.

2 CORINTHIANS 13:4

O Lord,
I know Your power is great. . .greater than any other source on earth.
Remind me when I feel weak today that Your strength is sufficient.
Amen.

Prayer

*Prayer is an indispensable part of
our relationship with Jesus Christ.*
LAUREL OKE LOGAN

If ye then, being evil, know how to give good gifts unto your
children, how much more shall your Father which is in heaven
give good things to them that ask him?

MATTHEW 7:11

And in that day ye shall ask me nothing. Verily, verily, I say unto
you, Whatsoever ye shall ask the Father in my name, he will give
it you. Hitherto have ye asked nothing in my name: ask, and ye
shall receive, that your joy may be full.

JOHN 16:23–24

But thou, when thou prayest, enter into thy closet, and when
thou hast shut thy door, pray to thy Father which is in secret;
and thy Father which seeth in secret shall reward thee openly.
But when ye pray, use not vain repetitions, as the heathen
do: for they think that they shall be heard for their much
speaking.

MATTHEW 6:6–7

Give ear to my words, O LORD, consider my meditation.
Hearken unto the voice of my cry, my King, and my God: for
unto thee will I pray. My voice shalt thou hear in the morning,
O LORD; in the morning will I direct my prayer unto thee, and
will look up.

PSALM 5:1–3

But we will give ourselves continually to prayer, and to the ministry of the word.

ACTS 6:4

Rejoicing in hope; patient in tribulation; continuing instant in prayer.

ROMANS 12:12

Evening, and morning, and at noon, will I pray, and cry aloud: and he shall hear my voice.

PSALM 55:17

He will be very gracious unto thee at the voice of thy cry; when he shall hear it, he will answer thee.

ISAIAH 30:19

Thou shalt make thy prayer unto him, and he shall hear thee, and thou shalt pay thy vows.

JOB 22:27

Praying always with all prayer and supplication in the Spirit, and watching thereunto with all perseverance and supplication for all saints.

EPHESIANS 6:18

I waited patiently for the LORD; and he inclined unto me, and heard my cry.

PSALM 40:1

And shall not God avenge his own elect, which cry day and night unto him, though he bear long with them?

LUKE 18:7

And all things, whatsoever ye shall ask in prayer, believing, ye shall receive.

MATTHEW 21:22

If my people, which are called by my name, shall humble themselves, and pray, and seek my face, and turn from their wicked ways; then will I hear from heaven, and will forgive their sin, and will heal their land.

2 CHRONICLES 7:14

Then shall ye call upon me, and ye shall go and pray unto me, and I will hearken unto you. And ye shall seek me, and find me, when ye shall search for me with all your heart.

JEREMIAH 29:12–13

The LORD is nigh unto all them that call upon him, to all that call upon him in truth.

PSALM 145:18

Let us therefore come boldly unto the throne of grace, that we may obtain mercy, and find grace to help in time of need.

HEBREWS 4:16

The sacrifice of the wicked is an abomination to the LORD: but the prayer of the upright is his delight.

PROVERBS 15:8

Ask, and it shall be given you; seek, and ye shall find; knock, and it shall be opened unto you: for every one that asketh receiveth; and he that seeketh findeth; and to him that knocketh it shall be opened.

MATTHEW 7:7–8

Pray without ceasing.

1 THESSALONIANS 5:17

And it shall come to pass, that before they call, I will answer; and while they are yet speaking, I will hear.

ISAIAH 65:24

Confess your faults one to another, and pray one for another, that ye may be healed. The effectual fervent prayer of a righteous man availeth much.

JAMES 5:16

And this is the confidence that we have in him, that, if we ask any thing according to his will, he heareth us: And if we know that he hear us, whatsoever we ask, we know that we have the petitions that we desired of him.

1 JOHN 5:14–15

Likewise the Spirit also helpeth our infirmities: for we know not what we should pray for as we ought: but the Spirit itself maketh intercession for us with groanings which cannot be uttered.

ROMANS 8:26

I will therefore that men pray every where, lifting up holy hands, without wrath and doubting.

1 TIMOTHY 2:8

I will pray with the spirit, and I will pray with the understanding also: I will sing with the spirit, and I will sing with the understanding also.

1 CORINTHIANS 14:15

Be careful for nothing; but in every thing by prayer and supplication with thanksgiving let your requests be made known unto God. And the peace of God, which passeth all understanding, shall keep your hearts and minds through Christ Jesus.

PHILIPPIANS 4:6–7

Oh that men would praise the LORD for his goodness, and for his wonderful works to the children of men!

PSALM 107:15

Yet the LORD will command his lovingkindness in the daytime, and in the night his song shall be with me, and my prayer unto the God of my life.

PSALM 42:8

Again I say unto you, That if two of you shall agree on earth as touching any thing that they shall ask, it shall be done for them of my Father which is in heaven. For where two or three are gathered together in my name, there am I in the midst of them.

MATTHEW 18:19–20

So that they cause the cry of the poor to come unto him, and he heareth the cry of the afflicted.

JOB 34:28

He shall call upon me, and I will answer him.

PSALM 91:15

Because he hath inclined his ear unto me, therefore will I call upon him as long as I live.

PSALM 116:2

Is any among you afflicted? let him pray. Is any merry? let him sing psalms. Is any sick among you? let him call for the elders of the church; and let them pray over him, anointing him with oil in the name of the Lord: and the prayer of faith shall save the sick, and the Lord shall raise him up; and if he have committed sins, they shall be forgiven him.

JAMES 5:13–15

Dear God,
I pray for my friends and family. Please protect them and help them to grow closer to You each day. I pray this for myself, also, Lord. I want to communicate with You continually, sharing from my heart, then quietly and patiently waiting for Your voice. Thank You, Father, for listening to my prayer. Amen.

Pride

Why are we not far more frightened of what pride can do?
Pride can cost us—and probably those after us.
BETH MOORE

And he said unto them, Ye are they which justify yourselves
before men; but God knoweth your hearts: for that which is
highly esteemed among men is abomination in the sight of God.

LUKE 16:15

Be not wise in thine own eyes: fear the LORD, and depart from
evil.

PROVERBS 3:7

And he sat down, and called the twelve, and saith unto them,
If any man desire to be first, the same shall be last of all, and
servant of all.

MARK 9:35

Surely God will not hear vanity, neither will the Almighty
regard it.

JOB 35:13

An high look, and a proud heart, and the plowing of the wicked,
is sin.

PROVERBS 21:4

Be of the same mind one toward another. Mind not high things,
but condescend to men of low estate. Be not wise in your own
conceits.

ROMANS 12:16

Talk no more so exceeding proudly; let not arrogancy come out of your mouth: for the LORD is a God of knowledge, and by him actions are weighed.

1 SAMUEL 2:3

The fear of the LORD is to hate evil: pride, and arrogancy, and the evil way, and the froward mouth, do I hate.

PROVERBS 8:13

Let not the foot of pride come against me, and let not the hand of the wicked remove me.

PSALM 36:11

Woe unto them that are wise in their own eyes, and prudent in their own sight!

ISAIAH 5:21

He that is of a proud heart stirreth up strife: but he that putteth his trust in the LORD shall be made fat. He that trusteth in his own heart is a fool: but whoso walketh wisely, he shall be delivered.

PROVERBS 28:25–26

But he that glorieth, let him glory in the Lord. For not he that commendeth himself is approved, but whom the Lord commendeth.

2 CORINTHIANS 10:17–18

How can ye believe, which receive honour one of another, and seek not the honour that cometh from God only?

JOHN 5:44

Pride goeth before destruction, and an haughty spirit before a fall.

PROVERBS 16:18

For I say, through the grace given unto me, to every man that is among you, not to think of himself more highly than he ought to think; but to think soberly, according as God hath dealt to every man the measure of faith.

ROMANS 12:3

But now ye rejoice in your boastings: all such rejoicing is evil.

JAMES 4:16

When pride cometh, then cometh shame: but with the lowly is wisdom.

PROVERBS 11:2

For if a man think himself to be something, when he is nothing, he deceiveth himself.

GALATIANS 6:3

Heavenly Father,
forgive me for my pride. I am no better than anyone, and You consider Your children as equals. I am humbled, Lord, that You have adopted me into Your family and call me Your friend. Amen.

Protection

God will never lead you where
His strength cannot keep you.
BARBARA JOHNSON

When thou passest through the waters, I will be with thee; and through the rivers, they shall not overflow thee: when thou walkest through the fire, thou shalt not be burned; neither shall the flame kindle upon thee.

ISAIAH 43:2

The LORD of hosts is with us; the God of Jacob is our refuge. Selah.

PSALM 46:7

In the fear of the LORD is strong confidence: and his children shall have a place of refuge.

PROVERBS 14:26

Be thou my strong habitation, whereunto I may continually resort: thou hast given commandment to save me, for thou art my rock and my fortress.

PSALM 71:3

But the LORD is my defence; and my God is the rock of my refuge.

PSALM 94:22

Above all, taking the shield of faith, wherewith ye shall be able to quench all the fiery darts of the wicked.

EPHESIANS 6:16

For thou, Lord, wilt bless the righteous; with favour wilt thou compass him as with a shield.

Psalm 5:12

The Lord liveth; and blessed be my rock; and exalted be the God of the rock of my salvation.

2 Samuel 22:47

Thou hast also given me the shield of thy salvation: and thy right hand hath holden me up, and thy gentleness hath made me great.

Psalm 18:35

The name of the Lord is a strong tower: the righteous runneth into it, and is safe.

Proverbs 18:10

Our soul waiteth for the Lord: he is our help and our shield.

Psalm 33:20

Every word of God is pure: he is a shield unto them that put their trust in him.

Proverbs 30:5

He shall cover thee with his feathers, and under his wings shalt thou trust: his truth shall be thy shield and buckler.

Psalm 91:4

But whoso hearkeneth unto me shall dwell safely, and shall be quiet from fear of evil.

Proverbs 1:33

The LORD is my rock, and my fortress, and my deliverer; my God, my strength, in whom I will trust; my buckler, and the horn of my salvation, and my high tower.

PSALM 18:2

And he said, The LORD is my rock, and my fortress, and my deliverer; the God of my rock; in him will I trust: he is my shield, and the horn of my salvation, my high tower, and my refuge, my saviour; thou savest me from violence. I will call on the LORD, who is worthy to be praised: so shall I be saved from mine enemies.

2 SAMUEL 22:2–4

The LORD is good, a strong hold in the day of trouble; and he knoweth them that trust in him.

NAHUM 1:7

Cast thy burden upon the LORD, and he shall sustain thee: he shall never suffer the righteous to be moved.

PSALM 55:22

For thou art my rock and my fortress; therefore for thy name's sake lead me, and guide me.

PSALM 31:3

God is our refuge and strength, a very present help in trouble. Therefore will not we fear, though the earth be removed, and though the mountains be carried into the midst of the sea; though the waters thereof roar and be troubled, though the mountains shake with the swelling thereof. Selah.

PSALM 46:1–3

The eternal God is thy refuge, and underneath are the everlasting arms.

DEUTERONOMY 33:27

The LORD also will be a refuge for the oppressed, a refuge in times of trouble.

PSALM 9:9

Dear Father,
thank You for Your physical protection as well as spiritual protection. There are so many occasions when I could falter, but You guard my feet. I trust You to protect me today. Amen.

Purity

*A person of purity stands before his peers and superiors
and courageously maintains his faith in God.*
CINDY TRENT

Drink waters out of thine own cistern, and running waters out of thine own well.

PROVERBS 5:15

Mortify therefore your members which are upon the earth; fornication, uncleanness, inordinate affection, evil concupiscence, and covetousness, which is idolatry: for which things' sake the wrath of God cometh on the children of disobedience.

COLOSSIANS 3:5–6

But fornication, and all uncleanness, or covetousness, let it not be once named among you, as becometh saints.

EPHESIANS 5:3

Thou shalt not commit adultery.

EXODUS 20:14

Lord Jesus,
*my thoughts and actions are impure at times. Please renew
my mind. Thank You for promising to forgive me
and consider me as white as snow. Amen.*

Repentance

*We long for revival, but revival
begins with repentance.*
NATALIE GRANT

Seek ye the LORD while he may be found, call ye upon him
while he is near: let the wicked forsake his way, and the
unrighteous man his thoughts: and let him return unto the
LORD, and he will have mercy upon him; and to our God, for
he will abundantly pardon.

ISAIAH 55:6–7

The Lord is not slack concerning his promise, as some men count
slackness; but is longsuffering to us-ward, not willing that any
should perish, but that all should come to repentance.

2 PETER 3:9

And the times of this ignorance God winked at; but now
commandeth all men every where to repent.

ACTS 17:30

I will have mercy, and not sacrifice: for I am not come to call the
righteous, but sinners to repentance.

MATTHEW 9:13

Remember therefore how thou hast received and heard, and hold
fast, and repent. If therefore thou shalt not watch, I will come on
thee as a thief, and thou shalt not know what hour I will come
upon thee.

REVELATION 3:3

Likewise, I say unto you there is joy in the presence of the angels of God over one sinner that repenteth.

LUKE 15:10

Or despisest thou the riches of his goodness and forbearance and longsuffering; not knowing that the goodness of God leadeth thee to repentance?

ROMANS 2:4

He that covereth his sins shall not prosper: but whoso confesseth and forsaketh them shall have mercy.

PROVERBS 28:13

Turn unto the LORD your God: for he is gracious and merciful, slow to anger, and of great kindness, and repenteth him of the evil.

JOEL 2:13

The time is fulfilled, and the kingdom of God is at hand: repent ye, and believe the gospel.

MARK 1:15

Repent ye therefore, and be converted, that your sins may be blotted out, when the times of refreshing shall come from the presence of the Lord.

ACTS 3:19

The LORD is nigh unto them that are of a broken heart; and saveth such as be of a contrite spirit.

PSALM 34:18

Repent therefore of this thy wickedness, and pray God, if perhaps the thought of thine heart may be forgiven thee.

ACTS 8:22

Draw nigh to God, and he will draw nigh to you. Cleanse your hands, ye sinners; and purify your hearts, ye double minded.

JAMES 4:8

Father,
I come to You to repent of my sins. Change my heart and my desires, Lord, so that from this day on I leave my sins in the past. Amen.

Rest

Again and again, I've found Him faithful to respond,
and the closer I move to Him, the safer I feel and the better I rest.
PATSY CLAIRMONT

Six days may work be done; but in the seventh is the sabbath of
rest, holy to the LORD.

EXODUS 31:15

It is vain for you to rise up early, to sit up late, to eat the bread of
sorrows: for so he giveth his beloved sleep.

PSALM 127:2

I will both lay me down in peace, and sleep: for thou, LORD,
only makest me dwell in safety.

PSALM 4:8

For he spake in a certain place of the seventh day on this wise,
And God did rest the seventh day from all his works. . . .
There remaineth therefore a rest to the people of God.

HEBREWS 4:4, 9

When thou liest down, thou shalt not be afraid: yea, thou shalt
lie down, and thy sleep shall be sweet.

PROVERBS 3:24

And thou shalt be secure, because there is hope; yea, thou shalt
dig about thee, and thou shalt take thy rest in safety.

JOB 11:18

He that dwelleth in the secret place of the most High shall abide under the shadow of the Almighty.

PSALM 91:1

Rest in the LORD, and wait patiently for him: fret not thyself because of him who prospereth in his way, because of the man who bringeth wicked devices to pass.

PSALM 37:7

Slow me down, Lord.
*My schedule gets so hectic that I find myself with my priorities
in the wrong order. Grant me a few moments of quiet,
so that I may collect my thoughts and be refreshed. Amen.*

Righteousness

We do not have to be qualified to be holy.
MADELEINE L'ENGLE

Blessed are they which do hunger and thirst after righteousness:
for they shall be filled.

MATTHEW 5:6

A righteous man hateth lying: but a wicked man is loathsome,
and cometh to shame.

PROVERBS 13:5

But seek ye first the kingdom of God, and his righteousness; and
all these things shall be added unto you.

MATTHEW 6:33

Lord, who shall abide in thy tabernacle? who shall dwell in thy
holy hill? He that walketh uprightly, and worketh righteousness,
and speaketh the truth in his heart.

PSALM 15:1–2

He withdraweth not his eyes from the righteous: but with kings
are they on the throne; yea, he doth establish them for ever, and
they are exalted.

JOB 36:7

Thy word is true from the beginning: and every one of thy
righteous judgments endureth for ever.

PSALM 119:160

Then shall the righteous shine forth as the sun in the kingdom of their Father. Who hath ears to hear, let him hear.

MATTHEW 13:43

The righteous cry, and the LORD heareth, and delivereth them out of all their troubles.

PSALM 34:17

Whereby are given unto us exceeding great and precious promises: that by these ye might be partakers of the divine nature, having escaped the corruption that is in the world through lust.

2 PETER 1:4

But if thou shalt indeed obey his voice, and do all that I speak; then I will be an enemy unto thine enemies, and an adversary unto thine adversaries.

EXODUS 23:22

If we confess our sins, he is faithful and just to forgive us our sins, and to cleanse us from all unrighteousness.

1 JOHN 1:9

Ye that love the LORD, hate evil: he preserveth the souls of his saints; he delivereth them out of the hand of the wicked. Light is sown for the righteous.

PSALM 97:10–11

And it shall come to pass, if thou shalt hearken diligently unto the voice of the LORD thy God, to observe and to do all his commandments which I command thee this day, that the LORD thy God will set thee on high above all nations of the earth.

DEUTERONOMY 28:1

Know ye not that the unrighteous shall not inherit the kingdom of God? Be not deceived.

1 CORINTHIANS 6:9

The eyes of the LORD are upon the righteous, and his ears are open unto their cry.

PSALM 34:15

The LORD will not suffer the soul of the righteous to famish: but he casteth away the substance of the wicked.

PROVERBS 10:3

Then shall thy light break forth as the morning, and thine health shall spring forth speedily: and thy righteousness shall go before thee; the glory of the LORD shall be thy reward.

ISAIAH 58:8

Blessed are they which are persecuted for righteousness' sake: for theirs is the kingdom of heaven.

MATTHEW 5:10

He that followeth after righteousness and mercy findeth life, righteousness, and honour.

PROVERBS 21:21

But know that the LORD hath set apart him that is godly for himself: the LORD will hear when I call unto him.

PSALM 4:3

The righteous shall be glad in the LORD, and shall trust in him; and all the upright in heart shall glory.

PSALM 64:10

Then shall he answer them, saying, Verily I say unto you, Inasmuch as ye did it not to one of the least of these, ye did it not to me. And these shall go away into everlasting punishment: but the righteous into life eternal.

MATTHEW 25:45–46

Dear God,
I want to seek after Your righteousness, following what is eternal and true. Thank You for Your faithfulness in the times that I seek to do right, even when I must stand alone. Amen.

Salvation

*Christ has made all things right. I had nothing
to do but accept it as a free gift from Him.*
HANNAH WHITALL SMITH

Therefore if any man be in Christ, he is a new creature: old
things are passed away; behold, all things are become new.

2 CORINTHIANS 5:17

Neither is there salvation in any other: for there is none other
name under heaven given among men, whereby we must be
saved.

ACTS 4:12

My little children, these things write I unto you, that ye sin not.
And if any man sin, we have an advocate with the Father, Jesus
Christ the righteous: and he is the propitiation for our sins: and
not for ours only, but also for the sins of the whole world.

1 JOHN 2:1–2

For this is good and acceptable in the sight of God our Saviour;
who will have all men to be saved, and to come unto the
knowledge of the truth.

1 TIMOTHY 2:3–4

But as many as received him, to them gave he power to become
the sons of God, even to them that believe on his name: which
were born, not of blood, nor of the will of the flesh, nor of the
will of man, but of God.

JOHN 1:12–13

He that believeth on the Son hath everlasting life.

JOHN 3:36

Jesus answered and said unto him, Verily, verily, I say unto thee, Except a man be born again, he cannot see the kingdom of God. Nicodemus saith unto him, How can a man be born when he is old? can he enter the second time into his mother's womb, and be born? Jesus answered, Verily, verily, I say unto thee, Except a man be born of water and of the Spirit, he cannot enter into the kingdom of God. That which is born of the flesh is flesh; and that which is born of the Spirit is spirit. Marvel not that I said unto thee, Ye must be born again.

JOHN 3:3–7

For he hath made him to be sin for us, who knew no sin; that we might be made the righteousness of God in him.

2 CORINTHIANS 5:21

But after that the kindness and love of God our Saviour toward man appeared, not by works of righteousness which we have done, but according to his mercy he saved us, by the washing of regeneration, and renewing of the Holy Ghost; which he shed on us abundantly through Jesus Christ our Saviour.

TITUS 3:4–6

Even as I please all men in all things, not seeking mine own profit, but the profit of many, that they may be saved.

1 CORINTHIANS 10:33

Lord,
what a sacrifice You made in sending Your only Son to die for me! It should have been me sentenced to that horrible death, but You saved me from the punishment that I deserve. Thank You for the free gift of salvation. Amen.

Scripture

*How much of a calm and gentle spirit you achieve, then,
will depend on how regularly and consistently, persistently and
obediently you partake of the Word of God, your spiritual food.*
SHIRLEY RICE

Therefore shall ye lay up these my words in your heart and in
your soul, and bind them for a sign upon your hand, that they
may be as frontlets between your eyes. And ye shall teach them
your children, speaking of them when thou sittest in thine
house, and when thou walkest by the way, when thou liest
down, and when thou risest up.

DEUTERONOMY 11:18–19

And that from a child thou hast known the holy scriptures,
which are able to make thee wise unto salvation through faith
which is in Christ Jesus.

2 TIMOTHY 3:15

For the word of God is quick, and powerful, and sharper than
any twoedged sword, piercing even to the dividing asunder of
soul and spirit, and of the joints and marrow, and is a discerner
of the thoughts and intents of the heart.

HEBREWS 4:12

God, who at sundry times and in divers manners spake in time
past unto the fathers by the prophets, hath in these last days
spoken unto us by his Son, whom he hath appointed heir of all
things, by whom also he made the worlds.

HEBREWS 1:1–2

That ye may be mindful of the words which were spoken before
by the holy prophets, and of the commandment of us the
apostles of the Lord and Saviour.

2 PETER 3:2

This book of the law shall not depart out of thy mouth; but thou
shalt meditate therein day and night, that thou mayest observe
to do according to all that is written therein: for then thou shalt
make thy way prosperous, and then thou shalt have good success.

JOSHUA 1:8

Let the word of Christ dwell in you richly in all wisdom;
teaching and admonishing one another in psalms and hymns and
spiritual songs, singing with grace in your hearts to the Lord.

COLOSSIANS 3:16

Thy word is a lamp unto my feet, and a light unto my path.

PSALM 119:105

So shall my word be that goeth forth out of my mouth: it shall
not return unto me void, but it shall accomplish that which I
please, and it shall prosper in the thing whereto I sent it.

ISAIAH 55:11

Searching what, or what manner of time the Spirit of Christ
which was in them did signify, when it testified beforehand
the sufferings of Christ, and the glory that should follow. Unto
whom it was revealed, that not unto themselves, but unto us
they did minister the things, which are now reported unto you
by them that have preached the gospel unto you with the Holy
Ghost sent down from heaven; which things the angels desire to
look into.

1 PETER 1:11–12

Thy word have I hid in mine heart, that I might not sin against thee.

Psalm 119:11

Heavenly Father,
I want to hide Your Word in my heart. Give me a clear mind as I meditate on scripture and memorize verses. I want to have Your Truth in the forefront of my mind, so that when I am faced with temptation or adversity, I can refute it with scripture as You did. Thank You for the joy that fills my heart as I reflect on Your Word. Amen.

Seeking God

*For it is impossible to be in the
presence of Jesus and not be changed.*
JOANNA WEAVER

But seek ye first the kingdom of God, and his righteousness; and all these things shall be added unto you.

MATTHEW 6:33

Sow to yourselves in righteousness, reap in mercy; break up your fallow ground: for it is time to seek the LORD, till he come and rain righteousness upon you.

HOSEA 10:12

Glory ye in his holy name: let the heart of them rejoice that seek the LORD.

1 CHRONICLES 16:10

And ye shall seek me, and find me, when ye shall search for me with all your heart.

JEREMIAH 29:13

One thing have I desired of the LORD, that will I seek after; that I may dwell in the house of the LORD all the days of my life, to behold the beauty of the LORD, and to enquire in his temple.

PSALM 27:4

With my soul have I desired thee in the night; yea, with my spirit within me will I seek thee early: for when thy judgments are in the earth, the inhabitants of the world will learn righteousness.

ISAIAH 26:9

And I say unto you, Ask, and it shall be given you; seek, and ye shall find; knock, and it shall be opened unto you.

LUKE 11:9

Seek the LORD and his strength, seek his face continually.

1 CHRONICLES 16:11

Seek the LORD, and ye shall live.

AMOS 5:6

Therefore came I forth to meet thee, diligently to seek thy face, and I have found thee.

PROVERBS 7:15

But if from thence thou shalt seek the LORD thy God, thou shalt find him, if thou seek him with all thy heart and with all thy soul.

DEUTERONOMY 4:29

If ye then be risen with Christ, seek those things which are above, where Christ sitteth on the right hand of God.

COLOSSIANS 3:1

Glory ye in his holy name: let the heart of them rejoice that seek the LORD.

1 CHRONICLES 16:10

They that seek the LORD shall not want any good thing.

PSALM 34:10

But rather seek ye the kingdom of God; and all these things shall be added unto you.

LUKE 12:31

If my people, which are called by my name, shall humble themselves, and pray, and seek my face, and turn from their wicked ways; then will I hear from heaven, and will forgive their sin, and will heal their land.

2 CHRONICLES 7:14

Lord Jesus,
I want to have a growing, vital relationship with You. Please don't let me fall into the complacency of having a stagnant relationship with You. I will only deepen my relationships with You and with others when I invest my time. Thank You for allowing me to come into Your presence and meditate on You. Amen.

Self-Control

Rules for proper behavior keep us from getting hurt.
We risk our own life and the lives of others when
we give in to our desires, whatever they might be.
LINDA BARTLETT

Then said Pilate unto him, Hearest thou not how many things
they witness against thee? And he answered him to never a word;
insomuch that the governor marvelled greatly.

MATTHEW 27:13–14

Yet Michael the archangel, when contending with the devil he
disputed about the body of Moses, durst not bring against him a
railing accusation, but said, The Lord rebuke thee.

JUDE 1:9

For even hereunto were ye called: because Christ also suffered for
us, leaving us an example, that ye should follow his steps: who did
no sin, neither was guile found in his mouth: who, when he was
reviled, reviled not again; when he suffered, he threatened not; but
committed himself to him that judgeth righteously.

1 PETER 2:21–23

Hast thou found honey? eat so much as is sufficient for thee, lest
thou be filled therewith, and vomit it.

PROVERBS 25:16

Charity suffereth long, and is kind; charity envieth not; charity
vaunteth not itself, is not puffed up, doth not behave itself unseemly,
seeketh not her own, is not easily provoked, thinketh no evil.

1 CORINTHIANS 13:4–5

Therefore let us not sleep, as do others; but let us watch and be sober. For they that sleep sleep in the night; and they that be drunken are drunken in the night.

1 THESSALONIANS 5:6–7

If the spirit of the ruler rise up against thee, leave not thy place; for yielding pacifieth great offences.

ECCLESIASTES 10:4

Let us walk honestly, as in the day; not in rioting and drunkenness, not in chambering and wantonness, not in strife and envying. But put ye on the Lord Jesus Christ, and make not provision for the flesh, to fulfil the lusts thereof.

ROMANS 13:13–14

Let your moderation be known unto all men. The Lord is at hand.

PHILIPPIANS 4:5

And beside this, giving all diligence, add to your faith virtue; and to virtue knowledge; and to knowledge temperance; and to temperance patience; and to patience godliness.

2 PETER 1:5–6

And every man that striveth for the mastery is temperate in all things. Now they do it to obtain a corruptible crown; but we an incorruptible.

1 CORINTHIANS 9:25

He sitteth alone and keepeth silence, because he hath borne it upon him. He putteth his mouth in the dust; if so be there may be hope.

LAMENTATIONS 3:28–29

Be sober, grave, temperate, sound in faith, in charity, in patience.

TITUS 2:2

Teaching us that, denying ungodliness and worldly lusts, we should live soberly, righteously, and godly, in this present world.

TITUS 2:12

But I keep under my body, and bring it into subjection: lest that by any means, when I have preached to others, I myself should be a castaway.

1 CORINTHIANS 9:27

Be grave, not doubletongued, not given to much wine, not greedy of filthy lucre.

1 TIMOTHY 3:8

Neither fornicators, nor idolaters, nor adulterers, nor effeminate, nor abusers of themselves with mankind, nor thieves, nor covetous, nor drunkards, nor revilers, nor extortioners, shall inherit the kingdom of God. And such were some of you: but ye are washed, but ye are sanctified, but ye are justified in the name of the Lord Jesus, and by the Spirit of our God.

1 CORINTHIANS 6:9–11

For if ye live after the flesh, ye shall die: but if ye through the Spirit do mortify the deeds of the body, ye shall live.

ROMANS 8:13

Dear God,

I need You to help me resist going along with the crowd when they do things that would displease You. Let my words and actions be a constant beacon, drawing the lost to You. Amen.

Sin

*It is the very nature of sin to prevent man
from meditating on spiritual things.*
MARY MARTHA SHERWOOD

Therefore if any man be in Christ, he is a new creature: old
things are passed away; behold, all things are become new.

2 CORINTHIANS 5:17

For I will be merciful to their unrighteousness, and their sins and
their iniquities will I remember no more.

HEBREWS 8:12

My little children, these things write I unto you, that ye sin not.
And if any man sin, we have an advocate with the Father, Jesus
Christ the righteous: and he is the propitiation for our sins: and
not for ours only, but also for the sins of the whole world.

1 JOHN 2:1–2

But if we walk in the light, as he is in the light, we have
fellowship one with another, and the blood of Jesus Christ his
Son cleanseth us from all sin.

1 JOHN 1:7

But he was wounded for our transgressions, he was bruised for
our iniquities: the chastisement of our peace was upon him; and
with his stripes we are healed. All we like sheep have gone astray;
we have turned every one to his own way; and the LORD hath
laid on him the iniquity of us all.

ISAIAH 53:5–6

Come now, and let us reason together, saith the LORD: though your sins be as scarlet, they shall be as white as snow; though they be red like crimson, they shall be as wool.

ISAIAH 1:18

To him give all the prophets witness, that through his name whosoever believeth in him shall receive remission of sins.

ACTS 10:43

This is a faithful saying, and worthy of all acceptation, that Christ Jesus came into the world to save sinners; of whom I am chief.

1 TIMOTHY 1:15

For this is my blood of the new testament, which is shed for many for the remission of sins.

MATTHEW 26:28

Who his own self bare our sins in his own body on the tree, that we, being dead to sins, should live unto righteousness: by whose stripes ye were healed.

1 PETER 2:24

Knowing this, that our old man is crucified with him, that the body of sin might be destroyed, that henceforth we should not serve sin. For he that is dead is freed from sin.

ROMANS 6:6–7

Who gave himself for our sins, that he might deliver us from this present evil world, according to the will of God and our Father.

GALATIANS 1:4

As far as the east is from the west, so far hath he removed our transgressions from us.

Lord Jesus,
I ask forgiveness for the sins that I've committed, even today. I repent of them now, asking You to help me leave them in the past. Nothing is worth separating me from You. I pray that You will give me the strength to defeat Satan and his attempts to keep me from living a life of victory. Amen.

Strength

*We must continue to ask God for wisdom and insight
and for the strength to persevere. He will cause us to rise
up and fly like eagles, walking and not fainting.*
NORMA SMALLEY

I know both how to be abased, and I know how to abound:
every where and in all things I am instructed both to be full
and to be hungry, both to abound and to suffer need. I can do
all things through Christ which strengtheneth me.

PHILIPPIANS 4:12–13

Finally, my brethren, be strong in the Lord, and in the power of
his might.

EPHESIANS 6:10

For the eyes of the LORD run to and fro throughout the whole
earth, to shew himself strong in the behalf of them whose heart is
perfect toward him.

2 CHRONICLES 16:9

Both riches and honour come of thee, and thou reignest over
all; and in thine hand is power and might; and in thine hand it
is to make great, and to give strength unto all.

1 CHRONICLES 29:12

By pureness, by knowledge, by longsuffering, by kindness, by
the Holy Ghost, by love unfeigned, by the word of truth, by the
power of God, by the armour of righteousness on the right hand
and on the left.

2 CORINTHIANS 6:6–7

He giveth power to the faint; and to them that have no might he increaseth strength.

ISAIAH 40:29

Wait on the LORD: be of good courage, and he shall strengthen thine heart: wait, I say, on the LORD.

PSALM 27:14

And he said unto me, My grace is sufficient for thee: for my strength is made perfect in weakness. Most gladly therefore will I rather glory in my infirmities, that the power of Christ may rest upon me.

2 CORINTHIANS 12:9

The LORD is my rock, and my fortress, and my deliverer; my God, my strength, in whom I will trust; my buckler, and the horn of my salvation, and my high tower.

PSALM 18:2

But they that wait upon the LORD shall renew their strength; they shall mount up with wings as eagles; they shall run, and not be weary; and they shall walk, and not faint.

ISAIAH 40:31

My flesh and my heart faileth: but God is the strength of my heart, and my portion for ever.

PSALM 73:26

That ye might walk worthy of the Lord unto all pleasing, being fruitful in every good work, and increasing in the knowledge of God; strengthened with all might, according to his glorious power, unto all patience and longsuffering with joyfulness.

COLOSSIANS 1:10–11

The righteous also shall hold on his way, and he that hath clean hands shall be stronger and stronger.

JOB 17:9

O God, thou art terrible out of thy holy places: the God of Israel is he that giveth strength and power unto his people. Blessed be God.

PSALM 68:35

The LORD will give strength unto his people; the LORD will bless his people with peace.

PSALM 29:11

Father,
*help me to see today how I can be useful. Then give me the strength
to walk into the opportunities You have set before me. Amen.*

Temptation

*Temptations come, as a general rule,
when they are sought.*
MARGARET OLIPHANT

Blessed is the man that endureth temptation: for when he is tried, he shall receive the crown of life, which the Lord hath promised to them that love him.

JAMES 1:12

The Lord knoweth how to deliver the godly out of temptations.

2 PETER 2:9

Because thou hast kept the word of my patience, I also will keep thee from the hour of temptation, which shall come upon all the world, to try them that dwell upon the earth.

REVELATION 3:10

Let no man say when he is tempted, I am tempted of God: for God cannot be tempted with evil, neither tempteth he any man.

JAMES 1:13

And lead us not into temptation, but deliver us from evil: For thine is the kingdom, and the power, and the glory, for ever. Amen.

MATTHEW 6:13

Watch and pray, that ye enter not into temptation: the spirit indeed is willing, but the flesh is weak.

MATTHEW 26:41

And when he was at the place, he said unto them, Pray that ye enter not into temptation.

LUKE 22:40

There hath no temptation taken you but such as is common to man: but God is faithful, who will not suffer you to be tempted above that ye are able; but will with the temptation also make a way to escape, that ye may be able to bear it.

1 CORINTHIANS 10:13

Thank You, Lord,
that You understand. Keep reminding me that You were in all ways tempted just like I am, yet without sin. It's so comforting to know that You have walked this same path and were victorious. Amen.

Truth

*If we are Christians, we have committed ourselves to
the Lord Jesus Christ who said, "I am the Truth."
In giving ourselves to Him, we dedicate ourselves
to the truth not only about Him but about ourselves.*
PAMELA HOOVER HEIM

God is a Spirit: and they that worship him must worship him in
spirit and in truth.

JOHN 4:24

Even the Spirit of truth; whom the world cannot receive, because
it seeth him not, neither knoweth him: but ye know him; for he
dwelleth with you, and shall be in you.

JOHN 14:17

Buy the truth, and sell it not; also wisdom, and instruction, and
understanding.

PROVERBS 23:23

For the LORD is good; his mercy is everlasting; and his truth
endureth to all generations.

PSALM 100:5

Jesus saith unto him, I am the way, the truth, and the life: no
man cometh unto the Father, but by me.

JOHN 14:6

He is the Rock, his work is perfect: for all his ways are judgment:
a God of truth and without iniquity, just and right is he.

DEUTERONOMY 32:4

Finally, brethren, whatsoever things are true, whatsoever things are honest, whatsoever things are just, whatsoever things are pure, whatsoever things are lovely, whatsoever things are of good report; if there be any virtue, and if there be any praise, think on these things.

PHILIPPIANS 4:8

And ye shall know the truth, and the truth shall make you free.

JOHN 8:32

That he who blesseth himself in the earth shall bless himself in the God of truth; and he that sweareth in the earth shall swear by the God of truth.

ISAIAH 65:16

For the word of the LORD is right; and all his works are done in truth.

PSALM 33:4

And for their sakes I sanctify myself, that they also might be sanctified through the truth.

JOHN 17:19

These are the things that ye shall do; Speak ye every man the truth to his neighbour; execute the judgment of truth and peace in your gates.

ZECHARIAH 8:16

Father,
You are the Source of truth. Teach me what is true concerning You, and give me the courage to seek the truth about myself. I am thankful that truth will triumph, and that the followers of truth will be victorious. Amen.

Understanding

*Yearn to understand first
and to be understood second.*
BECA LEWIS ALLEN

Happy is the man that findeth wisdom, and the man that getteth understanding. For the merchandise of it is better than the merchandise of silver, and the gain thereof than fine gold. She is more precious than rubies: and all the things thou canst desire are not to be compared unto her.

PROVERBS 3:13–15

The tongue of the wise useth knowledge aright: but the mouth of fools poureth out foolishness.

PROVERBS 15:2

Then shalt thou understand the fear of the LORD, and find the knowledge of God. For the LORD giveth wisdom: out of his mouth cometh knowledge and understanding.

PROVERBS 2:5–6

In the lips of him that hath understanding wisdom is found: but a rod is for the back of him that is void of understanding.

PROVERBS 10:13

When wisdom entereth into thine heart, and knowledge is pleasant unto thy soul; discretion shall preserve thee, understanding shall keep thee: to deliver thee from the way of the evil man.

PROVERBS 2:10–12

They shall not hurt nor destroy in all my holy mountain: for the earth shall be full of the knowledge of the Lord, as the waters cover the sea. And in that day there shall be a root of Jesse, which shall stand for an ensign of the people; to it shall the Gentiles seek: and his rest shall be glorious.

ISAIAH 11:9–10

If there be therefore any consolation in Christ, if any comfort of love, if any fellowship of the Spirit, if any bowels and mercies, fulfil ye my joy, that ye be likeminded, having the same love, being of one accord, of one mind.

PHILIPPIANS 2:1–2

When I was a child, I spake as a child, I understood as a child, I thought as a child: but when I became a man, I put away childish things.

1 CORINTHIANS 13:11

But thou, O Lord, art a God full of compassion, and gracious, longsuffering, and plenteous in mercy and truth.

PSALM 86:15

With the ancient is wisdom; and in length of days understanding. With him is wisdom and strength, he hath counsel and understanding.

JOB 12:12–13

And unto man he said, Behold, the fear of the Lord, that is wisdom; and to depart from evil is understanding.

JOB 28:28

Wisdom resteth in the heart of him that hath understanding: but that which is in the midst of fools is made known.

PROVERBS 14:33

The heart of the prudent getteth knowledge; and the ear of the wise seeketh knowledge.

PROVERBS 18:15

But as it is written, Eye hath not seen, nor ear heard, neither have entered into the heart of man, the things which God hath prepared for them that love him. But God hath revealed them unto us by his Spirit: for the Spirit searcheth all things, yea, the deep things of God. For what man knoweth the things of a man, save the spirit of man which is in him? even so the things of God knoweth no man, but the Spirit of God.

1 CORINTHIANS 2:9–11

Evil men understand not judgment: but they that seek the LORD understand all things.

PROVERBS 28:5

Folly is joy to him that is destitute of wisdom: but a man of understanding walketh uprightly.

PROVERBS 15:21

For if these things be in you, and abound, they make you that ye shall neither be barren nor unfruitful in the knowledge of our Lord Jesus Christ.

2 PETER 1:8

Make me to understand the way of thy precepts: so shall I talk of thy wondrous works.

PSALM 119:27

The rich man is wise in his own conceit; but the poor that hath understanding searcheth him out.

PROVERBS 28:11

Teach me good judgment and knowledge: for I have believed thy commandments.

PSALM 119:66

The heart of him that hath understanding seeketh knowledge: but the mouth of fools feedeth on foolishness.

PROVERBS 15:14

For to one is given by the Spirit the word of wisdom; to another the word of knowledge by the same Spirit.

1 CORINTHIANS 12:8

Justice and judgment are the habitation of thy throne: mercy and truth shall go before thy face.

PSALM 89:14

But let him that glorieth glory in this, that he understandeth and knoweth me, that I am the LORD which exercise loving-kindness, judgment, and righteousness, in the earth: for in these things I delight, saith the LORD.

JEREMIAH 9:24

Lord,

I often feel misunderstood. But thank You for understanding me.
Help me to turn to You, accepting Your will for my life.
When I can't understand Your plan, help me to trust in You. Amen.

Unity

The Word tells us that He has called His children to be one with Him and with each other. In order for His will to be realized, we must first unite. To unite simply means to join.
KATHERYN BOONE

Behold, how good and how pleasant it is for brethren to dwell together in unity!

PSALM 133:1

Now the God of patience and consolation grant you to be likeminded one toward another according to Christ Jesus: that ye may with one mind and one mouth glorify God, even the Father of our Lord Jesus Christ.

ROMANS 15:5–6

Be of the same mind one toward another.

ROMANS 12:16

Now I beseech you, brethren, by the name of our Lord Jesus Christ, that ye all speak the same thing, and that there be no divisions among you; but that ye be perfectly joined together in the same mind and in the same judgment.

1 CORINTHIANS 1:10

Like snowflakes,
Lord, Your children are so different. Nationality, personality, appearance, or talent make no difference with You. Your love is the same for each individual. May I treat everyone equally as You do. Thank You that we're all special in Your sight. Amen.

Wisdom

*Learning is not attained by chance, it must be sought
for with ardor and attended to with diligence.*
ABIGAIL ADAMS

A wise man's heart discerneth both time and judgment.

ECCLESIASTES 8:5

Say unto wisdom, Thou art my sister; and call understanding thy
kinswoman.

PROVERBS 7:4

Be wise now therefore, O ye kings: be instructed, ye judges of the
earth.

PSALM 2:10

Therefore whosoever heareth these sayings of mine, and doeth
them, I will liken him unto a wise man, which built his house
upon a rock: and the rain descended, and the floods came, and
the winds blew, and beat upon that house; and it fell not: for it
was founded upon a rock.

MATTHEW 7:24–25

Wherefore be ye not unwise, but understanding what the will of
the Lord is.

EPHESIANS 5:17

He that is void of wisdom despiseth his neighbour: but a man of
understanding holdeth his peace.

PROVERBS 11:12

A prudent man foreseeth the evil, and hideth himself: but the simple pass on, and are punished.

PROVERBS 22:3

The LORD by wisdom hath founded the earth; by understanding hath he established the heavens. By his knowledge the depths are broken up, and the clouds drop down the dew. My son, let not them depart from thine eyes: keep sound wisdom and discretion.

PROVERBS 3:19–21

I wisdom dwell with prudence, and find out knowledge of witty inventions.

PROVERBS 8:12

He that handleth a matter wisely shall find good: and whoso trusteth in the LORD, happy is he. The wise in heart shall be called prudent: and the sweetness of the lips increaseth learning.

PROVERBS 16:20–21

Who is wise, and he shall understand these things? prudent, and he shall know them? for the ways of the LORD are right, and the just shall walk in them: but the transgressors shall fall therein.

HOSEA 14:9

My son, attend to my words; incline thine ear unto my sayings. Let them not depart from thine eyes; keep them in the midst of thine heart. For they are life unto those that find them, and health to all their flesh.

PROVERBS 4:20–22

The law of the wise is a fountain of life, to depart from the snares of death. Good understanding giveth favour: but the way of transgressors is hard.

PROVERBS 13:14–15

For your obedience is come abroad unto all men. I am glad therefore on your behalf: but yet I would have you wise unto that which is good, and simple concerning evil.

ROMANS 16:19

And they that be wise shall shine as the brightness of the firmament; and they that turn many to righteousness as the stars for ever and ever.

DANIEL 12:3

How much better is it to get wisdom than gold! and to get understanding rather to be chosen than silver!

PROVERBS 16:16

With him is strength and wisdom: the deceived and the deceiver are his. He leadeth counsellors away spoiled, and maketh the judges fools.

JOB 12:16–17

My son, eat thou honey, because it is good; and the honeycomb, which is sweet to thy taste: so shall the knowledge of wisdom be unto thy soul: when thou hast found it, then there shall be a reward, and thy expectation shall not be cut off.

PROVERBS 24:13–14

And wisdom and knowledge shall be the stability of thy times, and strength of salvation: the fear of the LORD is his treasure.

ISAIAH 33:6

I will instruct thee and teach thee in the way which thou shalt go: I will guide thee with mine eye.

PSALM 32:8

If any of you lack wisdom, let him ask of God, that giveth to all men liberally, and upbraideth not; and it shall be given him.

JAMES 1:5

Howbeit we speak wisdom among them that are perfect: yet not the wisdom of this world, nor of the princes of this world, that come to nought: but we speak the wisdom of God in a mystery, even the hidden wisdom, which God ordained before the world unto our glory: which none of the princes of this world knew: for had they known it, they would not have crucified the Lord of glory.

1 CORINTHIANS 2:6–8

Whoso is wise, and will observe these things, even they shall understand the lovingkindness of the LORD.

PSALM 107:43

And if any man think that he knoweth any thing, he knoweth nothing yet as he ought to know.

1 CORINTHIANS 8:2

A good man sheweth favour, and lendeth: he will guide his affairs with discretion.

PSALM 112:5

For wisdom is a defence, and money is a defence: but the excellency of knowledge is, that wisdom giveth life to them that have it.

ECCLESIASTES 7:12

Lord Jesus,
You have promised that if I ask for wisdom, You will give it to me.
I ask for a sharp mind and sound judgment to be used for Your glory.
Amen.